6/25/12
#39.95

On CRIMES and PUNISHMENTS

On *CRIMES* and PUNISHMENTS

Fifth Edition

CESARE BECCARIA

Translation, Annotations, and Introduction by
Graeme R. Newman
University at Albany
and
Pietro Marongiu
University of Cagliari

Transaction Publishers
New Brunswick (U.S.A.) and London (U.K.)

Library of Congress Catalog Number: 2009000797
ISBN: 978-1-4128-1015-9
Printed in the United States of America

Library of Congress Cataloging-in-Publication Data

Beccaria, Cesare, marchese di, 1738-1794.
  [Dei delitti e delle pene. English]
  On crimes and punishments / Cesare Beccaria ; translated by Graeme R.
  Newman and Pietro Marongiu.
       p. cm.
  Includes bibliographical references.
  ISBN 978-1-4128-1015-9 (alk. paper)
     1. Punishment--Europe--Early works to 1800. 2. Criminal justice,
  Administration of--Europe--Early works to 1800. I. Title.

HV8661.B3 2006
364.6--dc22
                                                        2009000797

Contents

Introduction to the *Treatise*

The rays of the sun
Drive away the night;
Destroyed is the hypocrite's
Superstitious power.
—Sarastro in Mozart's *The Magic Flute*

What did you do to earn all this? You took the trouble to get born—
nothing more.
—Figaro denounces Count Almaviva in *The Marriage of Figaro* (from
the play by Pierre Augustin Caron de Beaumarchais, 1778; later
transformed by Mozart into his opera *La Nozze di Figaro*).

Beccaria wrote at an exciting time. The great Western philosophers
of the seventeenth and eighteenth centuries brought light to a world of
darkness; a world kept dark by religion and the privileges of noble rank.
Though it is difficult to settle on exact dates for the period of the enlightenment in Western thought, generally, it filled an exciting and at times
turbulent century from roughly the late 1600s to the late 1700s. But there
was no real beginning, rather a rediscovery and reinterpretation of the
legacy of the great classical thinkers of Greece and Rome, thinkers whose
ideas were, in large part, suffocated by several centuries of the Church,
especially soon after the renaissance ebbed away, lying dormant, wait-
ing rediscovery. The *Philosophes* of western Europe directly assaulted
the centuries old canon of privilege by birth. A self made man was to
be admired and deserved better. It was as though they were preparing
men for the industrial revolution that was just around the corner. And of
course, they embraced the principles of science, so ably expounded by
Bacon, whom Beccaria quotes at the beginning of the *Treatise*.

Nor has the enlightenment period really passed. Nineteenth-century
thinkers such as Darwin and Marx each logically extended the ethos of
the enlightenment—Marx with his critique of individualism coupled
with egalitarian advocacy, especially in his early writings, and Darwin
with a logical extension of the scientific ethos of the enlightenment that
did not doubt that it would overtake even the work of God. And the

twentieth century, perhaps the century of unbridled "enlightenment" saw Freud extend the iconic idea of the enlightenment, the pursuit of happiness—unhappily as it turned out—as the scientific basis for understanding all of human behavior. Yet Freud's insights provided the framework for the first concerted effort to disavow the enlightenment, with the writing of the *Dialectic of the Enlightenment* by Horkheimer and Adorno (2002) arguing that it had not set men free, but rather had set free their resentment and repressed violence, resulting in the genocidal acts of the twentieth century, especially the holocaust of World War II. Foucault took this further and argued that the enlightenment had not set man free at all, but had enchained him inside the unseen hand of social control, wrought by the increasingly alienating engines of technology and industry (Foucault, 1961, 1977).

But in America, the enlightenment is reaffirmed every day by a government and constitution that owe not a little to its revolutionary ideas.

It is against this rich tapestry that we must view Beccaria's *Treatise*. Beccaria has brought to bear many, perhaps all, the great ideas of the enlightenment thinkers on the problem of crime and criminal justice. In that sense, there is little in the *Treatise* that is original. Montesquieu in particular had written much about the origin and meaning of law as had Voltaire who not only wrote about the law, but also practiced it in a reformist manner. Beccaria's use of the many ideas of other enlightenment thinkers also makes for considerable difficulty in interpreting what he has written, because although all the enlightenment thinkers were driven by a dominant ethos of breaking away from the chains of religion and advocating free men and free minds, there was much disagreement as to how this might be achieved, especially on what an enlightened, "scientific" society would be like—except in very general terms, that is, the greatest happiness for the greatest number, upon which all agreed. The result is that the *Treatise* contains many passages that are ambiguous, and many passages that are contradictory.

Understanding the *Treatise*

There are three master themes of the enlightenment that run through the *Treatise*. These are the idea of the social contract, the idea of science, and the belief in progress. These are set within the context of a utilitarian view of society based on the greatest happiness for the greatest number, in turn based on a conception of human nature that was essentially hedonistic, that is, happiness was generally equated with pleasure and/or the avoidance of pain. The idea of the social contact forms the moral and political basis of the reformist zeal that exudes from the *Treatise*. The idea of science provides the dispassionate and reasoned appeal of the reforms; the belief in progress, inextricably bound to the idea of science, provides the necessary optimism for accepting Beccaria's proposals and at the same time a passionate critique and rejection of past practices. Many of the enlightenment thinkers were conflicted about their own arguments, so it is understandable that Beccaria may reproduce such ambivalence. Yet the tone of Beccaria's writing reflects little uncertainty. The *Treatise* is essentially an ideological tract designed to persuade its readers and even shock them where it is safe to do so.

The first five chapters: "To the Reader," "Introduction," and Chapters I through III set the political and philosophical groundwork for the rest of the *Treatise*. This ground is essentially that of the social contract, which is where we begin in this introduction for it is surely the lynchpin to the entire *Treatise*. It provides the theoretical basis and justification for the rule of law as we know it today. Without it, the right to punish dissolves. Without it, the law cannot exist. Indeed, without it, a society cannot be a society, at least according to the enlightenment thinkers. The necessity for the master concept of the social contract derives from the eighteenth century conception of the primitive state of nature inextricably bound to the great tradition of natural law. For, if humans naturally worked together with mutual interest in each other, law would neither be necessary nor justifiable. But if man[1] is a primitive, selfish being whose interests are in conflict with those of his brothers, then law is necessary and certainly justifiable if individuals are to be protected from each other. So the derivation of the concept of the social contract lies in the conceptions of man's original state of nature, his primitive state.

In what follows we provide just a small sampling of the body of works that lay behind the idea of the social contract as it is expounded, so briefly and superficially, in the *Treatise*. We cannot hope to cover all the controversies, digressions and evolutionary developments of social contract theory and its related issues that have occurred over its several hundred year's history. It is the story of the development of political thought that helped produce the democracies of various kinds as we know them today. If we manage to convey just how critical these ideas were to Beccaria's *Treatise*, and how incredibly relevant they remain to this very day we will have achieved much. The ideas underlying the social contract are played out and tested in every democracy every day of every year of their existence. As citizens of these democracies we suffer the imperfections of the theory, but also reap its advantages.

The Social Contract and the Primitive State of Nature

Beccaria clearly rejects Hobbes in his To the Reader when he notes, "It would be wrong, when speaking of the state of war that existed before society came into being, to assume that it was the Hobbesian state of nature bereft of any overriding human duty or obligation." This is indeed an accurate depiction of Hobbes who famously noted that nature endowed on man the "Right to everything; even to one another's body" (Haakonssen, 1996: 31), that in the state of nature life was "solitary, poor, nasty, brutish and short":

> *Jus Naturale,* is the Liberty each man hath, to use his power, as he will himselfe, for the preservation of his own Nature; that is to say his own life…and consequently of doing any thing, which in his own judgement, and Reason, he shall conceive to be the aptest means thereunto (Hobbes, 1991: 91).

But this apparent rejection of Hobbes should be seen against what Beccaria has put in its place. Beccaria's language throughout the *Treatise*, especially the assumption that human nature is driven by the pursuit of happiness, leads him by implication to take a similar view of the primitive state of nature. For Hobbes, the original state of nature is ordained by the right of individuals to be concerned primarily, indeed only, for their own survival. This was a "fact" and "right" at the same time as far as Hobbes was concerned. So humans had a right to defend themselves for just this one reason: survival. At the same time, though, men also pursued logically and mechanistically power as a means of ensuring their own survival. Beccaria's presumption of the pursuit of happiness by implication takes the Hobbes view much further: not only will men act to defend their survival, but they want much more: they want happiness which in Beccaria's conception (to be explicated much further by Bentham and others, see below) meant the pursuit of pleasure and avoidance of pain. Thus the "war of all against all" takes on a colorful, indeed outrageous proportion of violence in the pursuit of desire. It is a much more extreme view of the primitive state of nature than that of Hobbes. It might be added that Hobbes saw individuals as also pursuing peace—quite a different positive motivating human desire in contrast to "happiness" understood as pleasure.

However, in many other places throughout the *Treatise*, and indeed the general language used to describe human nature, it is clear that Beccaria also accepts Hobbes's view of human nature in its primitive state. Take for example, "The first laws and the first judges were born of necessity to give shelter against the disorder caused by the intrinsic physical despotism of every man," in Chapter IX, or the "inevitable evil of men" in Chapter XLII. At the same time he underplays the potentially limitless pursuit of others implied in the happiness principle: "Primitive man damages others only enough to satisfy his needs," without specifying what these needs are, which if they are happiness, are limitless.

Explicitly acknowledging Hobbes's view of the primitive state of nature poses a serious problem for Beccaria who embraces so completely the idea of the social contract. It forces Beccaria to recognize that social contract theory rests upon a difficult contradiction. For if humans are driven by instinctual desires, how are they able to think rationally beyond these desires? Surely to make any kind of contract requires men who can think and make a choice? Hobbes had no problem with this seeming contradiction. He flatly denied that there was any such thing as free will. Humans in the state of nature or anywhere else for that matter were moved by forces larger than themselves, like heavenly bodies and in geometrical fashion, very predictable. In order for humans to make choices they had to be forced to do so which was why, eventually, Hobbes proposed the Leviathan, the sovereign state, all powerful, to construct laws and make decisions to ensure the security of individuals in society. Hobbes, unlike Beccaria, was a radical. It is commonly overlooked that more than half Hobbes's *Leviathan* is taken up with cogent arguments against religion, developing his overall thesis that men cannot know the real world, that everything in it is a construction, including everything physical (the color red for example) let alone God. The irony is, though, that Hobbes also used as his starting point a theory that had offered a way out of the seeming contradiction that confronted Beccaria. This was natural law, the idea that men were born with certain ideas and "laws" embedded in them, the same kinds of laws that governed nature; the order of the universe.

The Social Contract and Natural Law

We can begin almost at any point of western thought to identify the idea of natural law. The ancient Greeks saw order (*Kosmos*) in the world around them, and Plato and Aristotle had much to say about them (Koenig, 2004: 1). The Romans continued this view and made more explicit the link between natural order and law. Cicero in his *De Republica* wrote, "True law is right reason in agreement with nature, it is of universal application, unchanging, everlasting; it summons to duty by its commands, and averts from wrongdoing by its prohibitions....Whoever is disobedient is fleeing from himself..." (Weinreb, 1987: 40). In this passage

Cicero lays out the view of natural law that would make it so relevant to humans and human society: humans are part of the natural order; they have internalized this order so that it is the natural thing to obey it.[2] According to the ancient Greeks and Romans, the order of the universe was in fact beyond the reach of mere mortals: catastrophes occurred about which humans had no control. The assumption was invariably that these catastrophes occurred because someone, somewhere, had disobeyed the gods—the natural order.

There are serious difficulties with this view of law, not the least of which is how one defines or characterizes "nature." Of particular difficulty was (and still is) the Stoic idea that all humans were alike, all expressed their part in nature. So a system of laws, formally written was not really necessary if every person had the capacity to understand his place in the order of things. This led to a strong equalitarian strain in the idea of natural law, in which it was assumed that all individuals were "equal before the law" equal, though, in the sense that the natural order included and affected them in the same way. This led to a rather difficult contradiction which was that humans then (and now) were not equal before nature, if one took as an expression of nature, the structure of society which then was divided into citizens and slaves. So the big question was how broadly does one define nature, and what in the natural order (or disorder) is man made, and what "natural"? The Romans, being a practical people, did not concern themselves too much with this metaphysical problem, rather they set out to develop a system of laws that worked for them and acknowledged the natural order. This began with a classification of law, the most widely used being that of Ulpian writing in the second century A.D. (Weinreb, 1987). He divided law into three categories: (1) *ius naturale* pertaining to humans and animals, including union of man and woman, marriage and procreation; (2) *ius gentium* pertaining to slaves, setting it apart from natural law—though there is an obvious contradiction with the inclusion of animals in natural law; (3) and *ius civile* pertaining to laws of the State.

Some centuries later, Thomas Aquinas realigned this classification of law with Christianity, distinguishing four types of law:

1.   eternal law the timeless divine plan of God, providence;
2.   natural law, the crux of Aquinas's system, in which man expresses his capacity to reason and think, capacities endowed by God (that is, he acts within eternal law); a tree loses its leaves in winter because it does, not because it must. A human reasons not only because it does, but because it *knows* it has reason and therefore *must* use it. Hence

the leap from "is" to "ought." Which makes natural order normative. Natural law is therefore man's moral compass, he must always choose, for example, good over evil;

3. human law, called positive law, derives specific laws from natural law, such as for example, one should not kill, or one should be punished for a specific act in a particular way. A law is unjust if it is contrary to human good;

4. divine law comprising the old and new testaments.

There is a serious difficulty embedded in this idea of natural law; a difficulty that has been with us at least since the Greeks. It is the role of reason: for how can man be both part of nature and yet separate from it by his capacity to reason, which is itself part of nature? Aquinas supplied a neat thirteenth-century Christian solution: since God is all good, anything evil must derive from good. Thus, the definition of evil, so well explicated by Dante in his *Divine Comedy*, early in the fourteenth century, is simply the perversion of good. Using similar logic, Aquinas derived positive (human) law from natural law and natural law from eternal law. Significantly, divine law was set apart from this syllogistic system of law. Positive law, therefore was at once guided by natural law, but always subject to human error. Yet this error would be of reason, which, it seems, in Aquinas's system was almost supreme. Unwittingly he had set the scene for later thinkers such as Grotius (see below) to supplant God with Reason in the explication of natural law. Even without Aquinas, it was inevitable that this should occur. Inevitable because of the natural order of things, and that most important element that has so far not even entered our discussion: the evolution of the concept of property, as a central feature of natural law.

Natural Law and Property

One of the few instances throughout Beccaria's text where he felt it necessary to revise his own words had to do with property. In Chapter XXII on Theft, he notes seemingly in passing: "... a crime of this unhappy part of men to whom the right of property (a terrible, and perhaps an unnecessary right) has left them a meager existence." In the first edition of the *Treatise* he had written, "a terrible but necessary right." In Chapter XXX he states: "The security of life is a natural right, the security of property is a social right" but in Chapter XXXIV he refers to the "sacred ownership of property," though stating, in the same chapter that "commerce and private property are not a goal of the social contract, but can be a means to obtain it." His confusion is understandable, since the evolution of the legal concept of property in natural law is subject to widely different interpretations, not the least by the two main exponents of the social contract in the enlightenment: Rousseau and Locke and their critic, David Hume, as we will see shortly.

We may begin with Grotius who is generally regarded as the father of the natural law concept of property. Grotius, writing early in the seventeenth century on the law of the sea, argued that the concept of property derived directly from nature, and that the concept of *private* property evolved directly from nature as it fashioned the social and economic relations among humans. Starting with the idea that in the primitive state of nature all property was common to all, everything there to be used by all ("universal use right"), but then private ownership evolved "not by a mere act of will, for one could not know what things another wished to have, in order to abstain from them— and besides several might desire the same thing—but rather by a kind of agreement, either expressed, as by division, or implied, as by occupation" (Grotius, 1625). To put it more clearly, private property had to evolve because of the inherent nature of much property: some things, for example, cannot be re-used once used, they are, instead, consumed. Thus, the idea that these could be available for universal use-right does not work in practice. In fact, a certain form of private ownership is inseparable from its use—something that applies especially to food and drink which are consumed, and are of course essential for survival. That universal and private use-right can exist side by side is explained clearly by Grotius's famous example of Seneca who said, "the equestrian row of seats belong to all Roman knights; yet the place that I have occupied in those rows becomes my own" (Buckle, 1991:13). Grotius continues to expound on the necessity, indeed inevitability, of any society to make clear distinctions between "what's mine" and "what's yours" (Grotius, 1625: Prol.5.):

> ... the maintenance of social order ... is the source of law... [which includes] ... abstaining from that which is another's, the restoration to another of anything of his which we may have, together with any gain which we may have received from it; the obligation to fulfill promises, the making good of a loss incurred from our fault, and the inflicting of penalties upon men according to their deserts.

This passage sums up pretty much the core of any criminal code as we know it today. Certainly, if compared to the last passage in Beccaria's *Treatise*, there is nothing in it with which Beccaria—indeed most people (unless they oppose punishment)—would disagree. What is surprising perhaps to the modern day thinker is that it derives from the idea of natural law. It is from this intellectual heritage that the modern idea of "inalienable rights" of man, and, thanks to the enlightenment, the idea of "individual rights" and modern rights such as the "right of privacy" spring. Beccaria, while he refers to natural law several times does not give it any special attention, though he did write that "Moral principles and political order come from three sources: revelation, natural law, and the accepted conventions of society" (To the Reader).

The direct link from Grotius to the enlightenment thinkers came through his defender and interpreter, Samuel Pufendorf (1672) whose work directly influenced Francis Hutcheson in Scotland as well as the French school. Unlike Grotius who took nature as eternal but not divine, and replaced God with Reason, Pufendorf, in his quest to establish the study of moral sciences, insisted that reason alone is not enough because it lacks moral power and therefore could not establish moral obligations. This view was later to be taken up by Hutcheson and by Hume in putting reason in its place, so to speak. It was the senses, they thought, that moved men, especially in the moral sphere, but also contributing to the sense data upon which scientific observations could be made. What was absent from Grotius, according to Pufendorf, was an understanding of the ways in which the natural law became part of human nature. Grotius assumed that these laws were "written in the hearts of men" at birth. Pufendorf insisted that these laws only appeared that way, but were in fact instilled into us from the moment we were born. As we would say today, it was the socialization process that produced these natural laws—but although these may seem variable, they were mainly the inevitable product of the necessities of social life, a product of the sociability of man (Buckle, 1991: 65). David Hume (1748) would take up this view in his critique of the social contract, and especially in his demolition of the idea of innate ideas in his *Essay On Human Understanding*.

One lingering question, perhaps doubt is a better word, remains concerning the ideas of all these thinkers about natural law, and indeed, law in general. Why is the concept of law so bound up in the maintenance of order? If man is so much like nature, why does he not act like animals in the wild, pursuing his own savage—or even refined—interests? This question hardly arose to the natural law theorists because they assumed that what was natural in nature was also natural in man. There was no conflict between the two, each was the expression of the other. Natural law expressed such harmony. But if that were so, why is it necessary to have laws that create obligations to make men obey? Shouldn't they do it without being told they have to? Pufendorf came very close to an answer: the natural sociability of man created this desire to live in harmony with others, to recognize others' property rights and so on. But the French *Philosophes* thought otherwise, especially Rousseau, with his picture of man being born free but then thrust into chains by the socialization process, buttressed by edifices of law, education, and commerce. So the question still remained, why must men be made to obey? And what is the justice of doing so? For as Horace wryly observed:

"And just from unjust Nature cannot know" (Buckle, 1991:18)

The Social Contract in the Eighteenth Century

At least three versions of the social contract were expounded in the enlightenment period. These were the theories of Locke, Rousseau, and Hume, each of these in various ways building on the venerable philosophical tradition of natural law but also very much informed by the genius of Hobbes whose idea of the social contract was couched, in part, in terms of natural law, although scholars have since concluded that his theory spelled the beginning of the end of natural law. Yet there is little doubt that Hobbes was considerably impressed by Hugo Grotius and by Pufendorf both of whom made the important advance in arguing that laws and morals were more or less human constructions.

Hobbes carefully coined his description of human behavior in the original state of nature in terms of humans' obligations, which he saw were confined only to themselves, and indirectly against others. The obligation was centered only on survival, a naturally limiting obligation (Tuck, 1991: ix-xlv). It was a right to defend one's self, not a right to pursue others, unless, and only unless, those others were threatening one's own survival[3]. The social contract that underpins law from both Beccaria's and Hobbes's point of view is *absolutely* necessary, to defend against utter violence and chaos. This conception of the original state of nature therefore justifies Hobbes's solution, which Beccaria clearly adopts, when he writes in Chapter I, "The sum of all these individual portions of liberty sacrificed for the good of all constitutes the sovereignty of a nation, of which the sovereign is the legitimate owner and administrator." Given his ambivalence about Hobbes as we noted above, one might ask, how did Beccaria end up so clearly endorsing Hobbes's idea of the social contract when he appears, in many places to reject it in favor of Rousseau, and possibly Locke, as other commentators on Beccaria have observed?

The three versions of the social contract on offer during the enlightenment period, each with their starting point of Hobbes and also in the venerable natural law tradition were those of Rousseau, Locke, and Hume. These were, respectively, the contract of society, the contract of government, and, well, no contract at all. These are theories about how any society may regulate the affairs of its citizens. They are at once attempts to explain how and why societies function given certain assumptions about humans and their sociability, and how much, if any at all, societies must impose on their citizens in order to function. We will begin by examining Rousseau, even though his work followed Locke's by some 80 years. The reason we begin with Rousseau is that, on a moment's reflection, we can see that in order to have a contract of government, there must be something with which government may make a contract, and that must be a society. It follows therefore, that a contract of society is logically antecedent to a contract of government. In other words, without a contract of society (that is, without a society at all) there can be no contract of government.

Rousseau and the contract of society.

If we are impatient with Beccaria's ambivalence about Hobbes and the primitive state of nature, we can perhaps understand it when we realize that Rousseau was himself deeply ambivalent about natural law. In fact, in an early version of his *Contrat Social* there was an entire chapter refuting the idea of natural law, but which never appeared in the final published book. Yet he took from natural law one of its essential tenets: the idea that all individuals were sovereign, in effect, each soul was special and was innately capable of knowing itself. And he turned this into a rabid individualism, putting him in good company with the likes of Hutcheson in Scotland, not to mention the strong idea of individualism and individual rights embedded in the natural law expositions of Grotius and Pufendorf. Rousseau questioned the original violent nature of man assumed in Hobbes's dictum, "man is a wolf to man" and rather complained that man's ills were thrust upon him by civilization's demands and oppressions, the errors of history as they were called by Beccaria (see Introduction, note 10). Thus, Rousseau's idea of the "noble savage," innocent and pure, unsullied by the evils generated by civilization became very popular[4]:

The opening sentence of *Contrat Social* has created the overwhelming conception of Rousseau as the great individualist, liberal to the extreme: "Man is born free and everywhere he is in chains" (Rousseau, 1947: 1; 1930). One may reasonably trace from this single sentence today's obsession with "individual rights"—rights that have been discovered in every corner of social and economic life. But if we look a little further to the last sentence of the first paragraph of Chapter 8 in Book I we find:

> "... man ought to unceasingly bless the day [i.e. the when the social contract was made] which freed him forever from his ancient state, and turned him from a limited and stupid animal into an intelligent being and a Man."

Rousseau was thoroughly torn. "He felt in his bones that the nation made law, and not law the nation," observes his incisive interpreter, Sir Ernest Barker (1960). Yet how could there be a formal, legal sounding thing such as a contract of society unless it was ordained by some kind of natural law embedded in nature? Furthermore, how could a society become a society when it was composed only of free thinking individuals? Natural law would say that they had common thoughts and interests, but its revisionists would say that their individual thoughts and interests must inevitably lead to conflict (as is implied in Grotius's view of property noted above). For how could each *individual* be truly free if he had to think like everyone else? One can see readily the impossible contradictions that Rousseau faced in trying to derive a form of government out of the romantic idea of individuals born free, full of rights, without obligations. The solution for Rousseau which he seems not to have followed, would have been to construct the idea of the original state of nature as one in which individuals were born with an inherent tendency towards sociability and cooperativeness. In this case, there would be no need for a social contract of society. Society would be self governing and self regulating. It would be a commune.[5]

But Rousseau did not take this route—most likely because it smacked so obviously of a natural law of inherent ideas. And in fact, if one conceives of nature as carefully ordered and orchestrated, it is quite logical to expect, as did the earliest natural law exponents, this order to also be innate in men.[6] The idea that men, even in the state of nature, possessed many positive traits that dispose them to work for the public good was advanced by Hutcheson (1755), who nevertheless was especially concerned that anarchy would arise without cooperative agreements among individuals. He argued that men, being rational, would recognize that they had more to gain than to lose by making such agreements.[7] But this is Hutcheson the realist speaking, not Rousseau the romantic.[8]

In fact, contrary to popular interpretations, Rousseau saw that the State (never clearly distinguished from "society") was the first hope for mankind: it could reach down and raise him up from barbarity. This is clearly the meaning of the quotation above. But what he does object to is a State based on usurpation of power or a patriarchal state (clearly objected to strongly by Beccaria). Its only basis could be that it was established according to the will of all—the "general will," as he called it. But the general will was not just the sum of all wills of every individual, it was a special kind of will, one that properly understood the common good. So important was the *quality* of this general will, as opposed to the *quantity* of wills, that it could only be conceived as being embodied in a few or even a single person—a legislator or ruler. This leads to an even more impossible contradiction. For Rousseau, given his high regard to individual rights will not entrust their rights to representatives (as in representative democracy) but only by direct democracy—that is direct votes by every individual. Unfortunately, if there is no State as yet formed, since it requires that in order to be born all individuals must surrender their own sovereignty (rights), then we have reached his famous paradox, for it turns out that Rousseau's citizens get nothing out of their surrender: "Each, giving himself to all, gives himself to nobody" (Barker, 1960: xlvi). Unlike Hobbes's individuals who surrender themselves completely to a Leviathan that is all powerful both as legislator and enforcer, Rousseau's individuals make a "contract of association." Rousseau insisted that "There is only one contract in the State, that of association, and it excludes all others" (Book III, c.16).

It is the general will of association wherein lies sovereignty and its only role is to make laws of a general kind. This idea stands or falls on whether or not the contract of association represents the real general will, a "true collective" rather than that of a collection of individual wills. Rousseau thought that the best indicator of whether the true will was represented would be the absence of factions and political parties. But the truth of the matter is that he could not trust people to make the right decisions. Rousseau says: "Of itself the People always wishes the good; of itself, it does not always see it" (Book II, c.6). There is here a clear parallel with Marx's famous notion of false consciousness, which, among other things, was used to justify the dictatorship of the proletariat. So unlike Locke, as we will see shortly, there was no room in the State of Rousseau for a permanent executive to actually enforce or administer the laws. Instead, it may establish a temporary government (small "g") which serves at the grace of the sovereign (general will). Again, we see a striking similarity between this theory of government (or construction of a government) with Lenin's dictatorship of the proletariat, a supposedly temporary State until the consciousness of the masses is brought into line with the collective will of the people (Lenin, 1918). Rousseau's solution is not a revolution, but instead he introduces a very old concept, dating back at least to Plato, that of the wise legislator who knows best. His contract of society, therefore, leads inevitably to totalitarianism since there is nothing in his theory to guard against the omnipotence of the ruler (*souverain*). In sum, Rousseau's is a "feel good" idea of the social contract that leads to the opposite of what he sets out to accomplish.

Locke and the contract of government—sort of

In Locke, we return to the line of argument produced by the natural law scholars. Being of Puritan stock, he accepted and sought to promote the great importance of the individual soul, and thus he championed the idea of individual rights. He also begins with a conception of the original state of nature, but unlike Hobbes who considered that there were no limitations on what an individual could or might do in the interests of his own survival, Locke argued that there were two inherent limitations to the rights of an individual to pursue his own interests: The first was that of private property of all—building on the ideas of Grotius outlined above—and the second, of great importance to criminal law and justice, that each individual had a right to punish those who broke the covenant of natural law. The latter idea is a slightly different way of restating Hobbes's view of the original state of nature that individuals would use their individual power to crush anyone who infringed on their survival. For Hobbes this was unbridled. For Locke, it is justified only when others transgress the natural law. However, it is on the issue of property that Locke's understanding of the social contract takes shape, for the challenge was to distinguish between common property and private property and what kind of agreement individuals could make about each.

Once again, the conception of the original state of nature is crucial. The assumption is that in its most primitive state there was no private property, indeed no property at all, unless one considers the earth, the stars, the moon, the total environment as being "property" common to all. Indeed, his was, roughly, the natural law view. But for reasons developed by Grotius and Pufendorf, private property evolved because of the logical demands of individuals living together. It was an inevitable and natural development of social and economic life. However, the implication for Locke and the natural law theorists before him was how would each individual defend his private property which was his right? So he has much more to defend than just his survival (which is all that Hobbes considered), he has his property as well. More seriously, since there was nothing in the natural law theory that said how much property an individual could accumulate, there is the problem of who has greater right to appropriate property that heretofore existed in common to all? And even worse, how could one justify the unequal appropriation of property if, as one would expect, some would end up with none or little property? This hardly matched the natural law tenet of the equal rights of all individuals. Why, then would individuals agree to preserve the private property of each individual? Much has been written about this issue and we cannot hope to resolve it in this brief Introduction. But the reader will recognize that this is a classic problem of economics and political theory that remains unresolved to this day, indeed over which revolutions have been and continue to be fought.[9]

The solution to this problem offered by Locke is neatly encapsulated by his idea of what property actually is. He argues that within each person lies his own property, "every Man has a *Property* in his own *Person*. This no Body has any Right to but himself. The *Labour* of his Body and the *Work* of his Hands we may say are properly his..." (*Two Treatises*, ii: 27). The young Karl Marx could not have said it any better. And it was on this very consistent view of individual rights held by Locke that he based his critique of slavery. So this does provide some inherent limits on the property one can accumulate—certainly one cannot own someone else. Slavery, therefore, is unjust. Furthermore, drawing on his Puritan heritage, Locke argues that the good work that individuals produce through their labor adds to the wealth of the community, and, given various inherent limitations on the accumulation of too much property by particular individuals (we need not go into the complicated details of his argument here) the challenge simply ends up how to make sure that the competition among individuals over property, motivated as each individual is by his own survival (a natural right as in Hobbes)—how can harmony be maintained? The solution parallels Hobbes. Locke states, "the great and *chief end* therefore, on Mens uniting into Commonwealths, and putting themselves under Government, *is the Preservation of their Property*" (*Two Treatises* ii: 124).[10] So we can see that it is both a point of rights and a point of expediency that individuals must join together to form a government.

Locke did not stop there. As we noted, he also argued that transgressors of natural law should be punished and by natural law we now also mean that the appropriation of another's property is an offence against natural law. The problem in accomplishing this task issues from Locke's general theory of human psychology (to be later extended by Hutcheson and others) which in some degree rests on Hobbes's argument that man can never know the physical world, that it is entirely subject to individual perception. Thus, Locke observed that when men judge each other they will naturally disagree and make mistakes. Furthermore, what is the point of making judgments about transgressions if there is no power to back up these judgments? That is to say, how does one legitimize punishment so that it is not, to use Beccaria's closing words to the *Treatise*, "an act of violence of one or many against a private citizen"? So there are sensible reasons to create a mechanism of government that lies beyond the special interests of individuals in society. These mechanisms turn out to be those that are now very familiar to us: a judicial system to administer law impartially, an executive to enforce the decisions made by the judicial system, and a legislature to enact uniform laws. In return for this service individuals give up their individual right to punish others since the mechanism of government does it on their behalf. It should be noted that this is vastly different to Hobbes who insisted that individuals gave up *all* their rights (except survival) to the sovereign. Locke is careful to preserve the right of property that is *not* given up to the government. He is also at great pains to spell out just what it is that individuals have agreed to in this social contract. It's a two step process.

The first contract is that of consenting to make "one community or government" (note that there is no distinction drawn between community or government at this point) "... and make one body politic wherein the majority have a right to act and conclude the rest..." (note his mention of the majority, a thorny problem which Beccaria does not seem to acknowledge in his wholehearted advocacy of the "greatest happiness for the greater number." See Beccaria's Introduction and Note 5). The second step, and overall the most important to Locke, was the investment of "supreme power" to the legislature. This was, however, a special kind of fiduciary power to act for certain ends, still reserving to the people the right to change the legislature and even remove it, should the legislative break the trust which the people have put in it. Much has been written on Locke's use of the word "trust" in describing the role of the legislature, especially the legalistic notions of trust as they are bound up in all sorts of contracts, dating back even to Roman Law (*mandatum*). But the conclusion we can draw from Locke here is that he had in mind a quite formal agreement. This is not an abstract theoretical idea of a social contract as expressed by Rousseau. The House of Lords in 1689, for example, even agreed by fifty-five votes to forty-six that there was an original contract between the king and the people. Locke no doubt was cognizant of this. So he had in mind the actual mechanics of formulating a social contract and it is clear that he was concerned not to give to the legislature too much power compared to Hobbes's Leviathan (which grabbed it all).[11]

Locke viewed the legislature as a beneficiary of the people's will, so technically speaking this was not really a contract between government and society. The only contract so far affirmed by Locke is the contract of society—that is, the people turn themselves into a combined corporate body and in that capacity establish the tripartite system of legislature, executive and judicial bodies. These bodies, especially the legislature have an obligation to fulfill their duties as defined from time to time by the corporate body. It is not a contract, rather it is an order given to the government by the people acting as a whole. This is entirely different to the conception of Hobbes who argued that the only kind of corporate body possible was a government (actually the sovereign signified in the person of the ruler or ruling body). Are we splitting hairs here? Maybe, but the resolution of this difficulty is crucial. Hobbes, very consistent on this, insisted that only the Leviathan could create a corporate body of an aggregate of citizens (just as only Leviathan had the power to create or take away private property). It was practically and physically speaking the only mechanism with the power to do so. Locke insisted that the power should remain with the people, which sounds much like Rousseau. We can see here that the problem comes down to how the power of the people gets translated into the power of the government while at the same time making sure that the government will not abuse this power and act according to its own interests rather than those of the people. The modern solution to this paradox is now well known: the separation of powers. We saw a glimmer of it in Locke's description of the government: consisting of three branches, and while he did not expound greatly on the importance of their separation of powers, Montesquieu had already advocated it as a means to provide a check on government running amok.

If Locke did not quite recognize the significance of his description of the government existing of three branches, this was perhaps the weakness in his theory of contract. But it also reveals his ambivalence, wanting to remain with the pristine—as later expounded by Rousseau—clarity of "all power to the people" when the people make their own pact and incorporate themselves as a body (a formal society one supposes) even dispensing with the mechanics of governing (but it is readily challenged with: what use is it then?) compared to establishing something practical that can actually execute the people's wishes—a government. While we may quibble whether this government served at the mercy of the people rather than made an agreement with the people to carry out its wishes (a contract) Locke's description of the mechanism of government makes quite clear that at least this was a way for a government to keep its part of the bargain (i.e., a mutual obligation that if the people give it power it would do as the people wanted). In our view, this amounts to something very close to a contract with government.

Hume: Where's the contract?

Hume, ever the skeptic, was prepared to accept that maybe government (more the *idea* of government) originated in consent, "somewhere in the woods and deserts," but he reduced the lines of argument supporting the idea to simply a matter of contemporary ideology of the political parties of England, the Whigs and the Tories which were but a hundred years old. In doing so, he appears to have simply ignored the long line of scholarship that we have outlined above in regard to the natural law origins of the social contract. Hume was a tough historian who demanded that the facts of history be acknowledged, and he pointed out— most persuasively—that he could find no government that was ever formed by such consent. In fact, just about all governments he could identify were established through usurpation, after which people were placed in a position of having to consent to the government ... or else. And even in those instances where consent was claimed, this was only a partial consent—including that of Athens taken to be the paragon of direct democracy, where he pointed out that only a very small minority (about one-tenth) of the people were asked to consent (slaves and women were not). So, even in cases that appeared to support the proponents of consent, he argued that these were invariably imperfect. Nor could he find any evidence that in cases where government was established by the smoothest process by succession (with less force, whether by marriage or inheritance, something of a parallel to the Divine Right origin of government) who nevertheless is in a position to consent to the change in government? To assume consent of every individual is utterly ridiculous as he demonstrates by his many caustic comments:

> "We may as well assert that a man, by remaining in a vessel, freely consents to the dominion of master; though he was carried on board while asleep, and must leap into the ocean and perish, the moment he leaves her" (Barker, 1960: 222).

Yet against his powerful dissection of the inadequacy of the philosophical idea (as he called it) of the original contract, Hume, the realist, understands that without something like it, there would be no stability and no security. As he notes:

"Did one generation of men go off stage at once, and another succeed, as is the case of silkworms… choose their government … establish their own form of civil polity without regard to laws or precedents which prevailed among their ancestors. But human society is in perpetual flux … it is necessary in order to preserve stability in government, that the new brood should conform themselves to the established constitution…" (Barker 1960:223).

This realism is echoed by Beccaria when he states in Chapter II, "The Right to Punish":

No man has ever freely given up a part of his personal liberty for the public good. Such a chimera exists only in novels. If it were possible, every one of us would wish that the agreements that bind other men did not bind ourselves.

In the long run, after his devastating critique of the idea of the social contract, Hume seems to end in a whimper with a conclusion that sounds most unsatisfactory. The idea of the social contract he views as a claim that the people consent to a government by making a promise that they will give it allegiance. He insists that there is no clear example in history of any allegiance given by people to a government on the basis of keeping a promise. In contrast, there is plenty of reason for people to give their allegiance to a government—any kind of government— "Because society could not otherwise subsist." This is a simple acknowledgement of the facts which any person, "even a lowly peasant" could understand. That all people would consent to a government based on the abstract idea of keeping a promise (the essential element of a contract), he says is simply beyond ordinary people's understanding except, maybe, philosophers. The bottom line is that any government is better than none, since it guarantees some stability in the everyday lives of individuals.[12] It is a supremely utilitarian view of society, Machiavellian in its cynicism, though viewing society from the bottom up rather than from the Prince down.

If we accept Hume's cynicism, much of the reformist basis of Beccaria's *Treatise* falls away, for its moral appeal rests almost entirely on his conception of the social contract. We are left with, perhaps, an admirable statement of ideals, rather like the appeal of Rousseau. If this is the case we should be wary of where Beccaria's embrace of utilitarianism will lead us (see below). For the moment, though, the utilitarianism advanced by Beccaria is very much embedded in the idea of science as it was conceived during the enlightenment period, and science does offer through Beccaria one appealing value in regard to criminal justice, that of impartiality or objectivity.

The Science of Man and Society

Beccaria writes at a point in the enlightenment of the eighteenth century when the discoveries of science seemed incredible (and they were) and the link between man and society was first clearly recognized as a problem that could be analyzed and understood by science. In fact, detached analysis of man and society was virtually the dominant ideology of the eighteenth century (Gouldner, 1970: 102-108).[13]

The dominance of the science of man and society is reflected in the *Treatise* through five interrelated themes which are derived in various ways from the dominant enlightenment thinkers: radical utilitarianism, determinism, observation based on the senses, economic analysis and finally of course, reason. The roots of all these ideas of science can be traced back way beyond the enlightenment period, at least as far as classical Greece (Newman and Marongiu, 1997; Marongiu and Newman, 1997). However, the idea of the objective analysis of man and society emerged just before the enlightenment with startling clarity. This was Machiavelli's *The Prince,* in 1532 which analyzed political society, especially the role of the sovereign in relation to his subjects, with a particularly detached utilitarian twist. So Beccaria adds to a definite Italian intellectual tradition.

Beccaria's embrace of utilitarianism is apparent on every page, and expressed in the epithet "the greatest good for the greater number" (an expression with inherent difficulties of interpretation, but its utilitarian logic is unequivocal). This approach to analysis allows its user to focus on consequences of action, which Beccaria uses with great effect as he forcefully demonstrates the negative consequences of unbridled judicial discretion, of torture when used in interrogation, and of the consequences of a sovereign ruling for himself rather than for his subjects. The right to punish does not derive from the right of a monarch or ruler—that is, the status into which he is born—but on an analysis of whether the punishment is absolutely necessary in a given case at a given time, what effects it will have on the citizens. Beccaria's assessment of the role of punishment is always a means-end analysis, even when he adopts a retributive position (see below). It was his utilitarianism more than anything else that endeared him to Bentham, and it had been adopted by many of the *Philosophes* of the enlightenment.

Though not essential to utilitarianism, it is an easy step to determinism from utilitarian logic. Because of the means end schema, the link between cause and effect is a necessary condition of any scientific endeavor. This may seem obvious today, but it was certainly not so during the enlightenment period among those who defended religious dogma and feudal structure of society. Had it been so, the likes of Voltaire would not have found it necessary to challenge through their actions as well as their words the abuses of logic indulged in by courts and magistrates whose procedures and laws were intertwined with the Christian and feudal views of the world. Theirs was a narrowly conceived determinism that all was ordained, and therefore determined by God, and the clergy retained for themselves the special privilege of identifying the causal path. The scientific concept of cause and effect instead allows for multiple causes and multiple effects, a far more complex arrangement. This makes for a much more complicated view of the world, especially of man in society, so it is not surprising that it met with such strong resistance from the church and others of privilege. This is why in many passages Beccaria often indulges in abusive ranting against those who he imagines are his opponents (see, for example, Chapter XXXVII and note 3).

In a complex world of multiple causes, external observation based on the senses (that is, the collection of data based on observation, the cornerstone of modern scientific method) is essential. Possibly, Montesquieu stands as the example of this approach, especially with his *Spirit of Laws*, a groundbreaking study of comparative law and society across many different nations. This study embraced the idea of multiple causes, demonstrating that law and social structure were relative to different conditions, supported by his observation of differences, a cornerstone of modern science. Beccaria was probably influenced by Montesquieu more than any other contemporary. He acknowledges this new scientific approach to the study of man in society when he notes in his Introduction: "We are now able to identify the specific links between sovereign and subject, and among nations," and "Certainly, laws have never been constructed according to the scientific study of human nature, which would comprehend in totality the actions of the multitude of individuals in society."

Also in the Introduction Beccaria introduces the first of his many suggestions for an economic analysis of man in society using language that bears a striking similarity to that of Adam Smith.[14] One of many examples of this language is found in Chapter XXXII:

> For men are more independent when under less scrutiny, and under less scrutiny when they are more numerous. But where the population grows at a greater rate than its country's borders, luxury is at odds with despotism because of the spirit of industry and the activity of men.[15]

Finally, the overwhelming theme that embraces all of the above themes is reason. While the great thinkers of the enlightenment disagreed considerably among each other as to how society was and should be formed and governed, they were all driven by one absolute (well, not quite absolute since Hume remained a skeptic) belief which was the superiority of reason. This was an incredibly optimistic view of the world, that reason would solve all the ills of society and mankind. It underpinned all of science and its absolute embrace, some would say, led to actions that were later regretted, such as the blood that flowed in the French revolution. It was also bound up in the romantic idea of progress, which we will consider shortly.

For Beccaria reason provided the framework for a mathematical way of analyzing human behavior and society. His nascent theory of society and politics is revealed in the essentially mathematical assessment of population in the quotation above. But it is also revealed in his transformation of the social contract into a formula: *la massima felicità divisa nel maggior numero,* (the greatest happiness for the greater number). The origins of the specific language of this idea are not certain, though it probably came from Beccaria's friend and mentor Pietro Verri (Bellamy et al., 1995: xix). The mathematical-like statement, the idea of happiness being divided in a concrete way probably comes from Hutcheson and/or Locke, both of whom were attracted to a mathematical analysis of social life.[16] The big question, still unresolved to this day is: what is the acceptable portion of society (if any) that may not partake of this happiness? Did Beccaria mean the greatest happiness for each and every individual, understanding that, under the social contract, each individual gives up only the smallest amount of his "happiness" needed in order to live in a secure society? (Bellamy et al., 1995: xx). We saw in the review of the social contract theories of Rousseau, Locke and Hume that this issue was never resolved, in fact from Hume's perspective it could never be resolved in the real world and could remain only a dim, romantic hope.

Finally, and perhaps paradoxically, the view of human behavior as motivated by pleasure and avoidance of pain Beccaria managed to encapsulate into his idea of reason. We say paradoxically because one would have thought that, within such a view of human behavior coupled with determinism, humans would behave according to these powerful emotions, thus eliminating any semblance of free will. Yet one would have thought that free will was a cornerstone of reason. The problem is solved by Beccaria and his contemporaries by arguing that the only rational action is that which comprehends the pleasure/pain principle.

That is, if one does not pursue pleasure and avoid pain, one is acting irrationally. So, the pleasure-pain calculus (as it came to be called by Bentham) neatly defines what rationality is and at the same time acknowledges its limitations (Newman and Marongiu, 1997; Marongiu and Newman, 1997). Everything that Beccaria says about the effects of punishment is based on this formula, though nowhere in the *Treatise* does he define the word "punishment" since, one suspects, he assumes that it is obvious: the intentional infliction of pain on a subject.[17] This view of human behavior, indeed human psychology, was later transformed by Sigmund Freud into the most influential psychological theory of the twentieth century, a theory that examined the intricacies of gratification and their links to reason and control. In many places, Beccaria anticipates this work, such as for example, "Not big speeches, strong words, or even the most sublime truths are enough over any considerable length of time to quell the passions excited by the demand for immediate gratification." The direct link between a crime and its punishment is therefore absolutely necessary according to this theory of human behavior.[18]

The Belief in Progress

The idea that one could apply the tenets of science, objective analysis, value free, to the study of society, humans and how they related to each other led easily to the idea that, if applied, it would naturally lead to a "scientific society" a society constructed by and operating upon scientific principles. This offered a new way to study an old problem: the idea of progress. The optimism is expressed by Beccaria in his Introduction: "Certainly, laws have never been constructed according to the scientific study of human nature.... If it were so, one clear proposition would follow: the greatest happiness for the greatest number."

Behind this statement lies an assumption about the inevitable evolution from simple and primitive, to something better, more advanced and refined. The enlightened thinkers had no doubt about this: they saw an evolution of law (the history of natural law), or morals and of science to be key to their understanding of contemporary problems. Armed with this knowledge they could demolish everything that they saw as archaic and no longer valid in an enlightened age. Certainly, they were convinced that their achievement of separating morality from religion and from law, in developing a science of morals as especially the Scottish philosophers did, from Hutcheson (1725, 1755), through to the early modern psychology of McDougal, was clear proof of such progress.

Beccaria's view of societal progress reflects especially the writings of the economist Turgot[19] (1913) and statistician Condorcet[20] (1804) both writing in roughly the same period as Beccaria. These writers, in different ways, built on the ideas of progress advanced by Aristotle and later by St. Augustine. The presumption was that humanity and society were conceived of as a kind of abstract entity, developing through very small increments and according to a set pattern. The assumed normal passage of history proceeded from barbarity to a general state of perfection (sometimes called happiness). Their evidence for this progress was gleaned from observation of foreign tribes and societies existing both before and in their day, to whom they ascribed the status of being less developed, or stuck at certain stages of development. Hume (Teggart, 1949) strongly rejected the French idea of social change, instead arguing for a general inertia as more characteristic of human societies. Ferguson (1782) later also advanced the stagnation view of progress in his *Essay on the History of Civil Society*. Ferguson was also influenced by Montesquieu who was clearly of the opinion that the great events in history (e.g., the fall of Rome) were caused by factors that lay beyond the actions of single individuals. If Caesar and Pompeus had not existed, other individuals and events would have emerged and contributed to the fall of Rome.

Our reading of Beccaria's view of history suggests that he is a little more inclined to believe that individuals, at least well educated intellectuals (following Rousseau and of course, Plato's philosopher king) could change the course of history.[21] But overall his optimism is clearly that of the French belief in progress towards an enlightened scientific society which was the beginning of a long line of French scholarship expressing this belief. The work of Saint-Simon emerged towards the end of the eighteenth century advanced the idea of scientific progress of society, and was developed by his student August Comte, regarded today as the father of the modern science of sociology (Bierstedt, 1978: 3-37). Emile Durkheim (1915) who wrote his dissertation on Montesquieu, followed this tradition, not only establishing sociology as a field of scientific study, but expounding the idea that society developed through stages from the primitive (*The Elementary Forms of Religious Life*), to the religious and ultimately to the scientific society, each stage exemplifying specific forms of social organization, such as for example, mechanical and organic solidarity (*Division of Labor in Society*). The idea of a scientific society and the method of obtaining it would eventually dominate modern sociology, and from it, in the United States at least, would emerge modern criminology and criminal justice. The method became known as "positivism," in sociology, the objective, empirical study of society.

Other Influences of Enlightenment Thinkers

Much scholarly gamesmanship has been devoted to searching out who had what influence on various aspects of the *Treatise*. Clearly, Beccaria's work is not "original" since it reflects many ideas well established prior to his writing. Whose ideas and in what sequence is anybody's guess, and a question probably not worth the effort to answer. What are important today are the ideas themselves, their development and their application. However, the works of Beccaria's contemporaries do provide the context for his own work, so in what follows we briefly summarize some of the main ideas and themes of leading enlightenment thinkers that are reflected in the *Treatise*. Since all of these thinkers also borrowed from each other, it is only in a general sense that we can claim to attribute the various ideas specifically to the thinkers, and it is even more difficult to assume that they were systematically imported by Beccaria into his works. Indeed, given the manner in which the *Treatise* was written (see Note on the Text), any importation of the ideas of others was most likely a haphazard process.

Montesquieu

Montesquieu is the only *Philosophe* mentioned by name in the *Treatise*. In his *Persian Letters* (1901), published about twenty years before Beccaria's *Treatise*, Montesquieu had harshly attacked the excesses of religion and in particular the inquisition. In fact he left no institution untouched by his scathing analysis, with the one exception of the family. The criticisms were based, essentially, on his view of society ruining the lives of men through the abuse of power by a few. More importantly, Montesquieu is probably the best example of the enlightenment thinker who truly implemented in his work the scientific method, which was to situate his ideas in the real world. He wrote extensively on the origins and functions of laws in society and in his discursive and incredibly disorganized *The Spirit of Laws* (1748) he tried to explain the causes and functions of laws and customs in various nations, how and why they arose, why the people in different nations did things differently. The major factor that contributed to the different "temperament" of nations, he claimed, was climate. And in turn, it was different temperaments that affected the origins and forms of laws and customs. This was a pioneering work of comparative sociology and comparative law. He also advocated a number of changes in the field of criminal justice that are very similar to those advocated by Beccaria: the simplification of law, the use of mild punishments, the abolition of violent punishments, the proportion between punishments and crimes and the abolition of torture, and the separation of criminal law from religion, especially the prosecution of religious offences (Beirne, 1983: 52). Montesquieu also gave a special meaning to the idea of a "social contract" which he used to defend suicide on the ground that no individual ever made an agreement to be born, so he had the right to end his life.

Voltaire

Many of the *Philosophes* were, and are, recognized social reformers, of whom the most famous is Voltaire. By "reformers" we mean that they were the most outspoken of the intellectuals in their criticism of the status quo, in their advocacy of change, and brave enough to accept the consequences of their activism—often banishment or prison. Voltaire, a rich noble in his own right, suffered at the hands of the authorities on many occasions. He was arrested, jailed and forced into exile as a result of many of his writings and plays.

The breadth and depth of Voltaire's writings are tremendous. When he turned his attention to questions of criminal law reform, he developed a unique strategy. His technique was to take up the cause of particular legal cases, and fight them publicly. The most famous case he argued was that of the execution of Jean Calas by breaking on the wheel. Calas had been convicted of murdering his father who had in actual fact committed suicide. Voltaire claimed a clear perversion of justice in this case. His relentless campaign eventually succeeded, and the sovereign was forced to restore the family honor of Calas. Voltaire turned this and other cases into public issues. To influence the virtually all-powerful sovereigns to intervene in this and other cases by using what amounted to "public pressure" as we would call it today was no small feat in the eighteenth century. Voltaire was the quintessential reformer—quite a contrast to Beccaria who had to be cajoled and pushed into writing anything at all, including the *Treatise* (Cantu, 1862: 149). Only after the *Treatise* became popular and widely accepted by a number of influential kings and queens, did Beccaria consent to publish the document in his name.

The fact remains though, that the ideas in the *Treatise* quickly penetrated the criminal laws, debates about penology and criminology throughout Europe, England and the United States. Maestro (1973) shows clearly that this would not have happened without the strong advocacy of his views by Voltaire, perhaps the most influential reformer of the period. Beccaria's views were almost a perfect fit to Voltaire's. The preamble to the *Treatise* established a view of the role of religion almost identical to Voltaire's: it should have a role, but not an all pervasive one, and certainly not fanatical. He sought to separate crime from morality. Beccaria's ideas on the role of the sovereign were also similar to Voltaire's: he recommended a carefully reserved role for sovereigns. Beccaria attacked the judiciary, not the sovereignty.

Helvétius

Several translators of the *Treatise* have noted the similarity of Beccaria's ideas on justice and the reduction of morality to the pursuit of happiness to Helvétius (see: Young, 1986: 84, 86). However, Helvétius, a controversial figure among the *Philosophes*, was far more radical or at least explicitly radical in his writings than was Beccaria, and he paid dearly for it. With the publication of *De L'esprit*, he at first recanted much of the content when charged by the Catholic Church with blasphemy, and was assisted by Voltaire to go into exile until things cooled off.[22] Of course, in his later writings he did not recant any of the ideas. If anything, they were even more extreme. There are three essential features of Helvétius' ideas that are of considerable relevance to Beccaria's *Treatise*. First and perhaps the most important was his thorough going hedonism which he called "self love" and for which he was often excoriated by many of his *Philosophe* associates, including Voltaire. "Self love makes us totally what we are. Why are we so covetous of honours and dignities? Because we love ourselves and desire our own happiness, and consequently the power of procuring it…. Power is the only object of man's pursuit" (Helvétius, 1777, Vol.1: 289-290). As we noted earlier, Beccaria stayed with the word "happiness" which is a sanitized form of the idea propounded in Helvétius of the pleasure principle: the pursuit of pleasure and avoidance of pain. It was the foundation upon which Bentham would later develop his entire system of morals and legislation. But Helvétius did not stop there. Since all the affairs of men were driven by self love, so also were the affairs of the Church against which he relentlessly applied his utilitarian ideas of morality, thus laying bare the crass motives of power that drove the church in all its works. This meant that the priests invented "crimes that honest men were likely to commit" (Helvétius, 1777: Vol.1. 220) in order to shore up the power and authority of the church. And, since much of the church dogma was directed at oppressing the pursuit of pleasure and self love, these were false laws creating false crimes, serving no public utility. When Beccaria refers to "bad legislation" and false methods of applying them he is very likely referring to this radical position of Helvétius.

The second significant idea was that of utilitarianism. For, if we are all driven by self love, it follows that societies should be organized accordingly to provide the maximum amount of self love for all. Hence, laws should only be made in so far as they acknowledge and promote this view of human nature. Fortunately, Helvétius also claims that one part of self love is security and, conveniently, conformity to the social order. Thus, in contrast to Beccaria's view of the social contract, he argues that the good citizen is "… not he who sacrifices his pleasures … to the public welfare, since it is impossible that such a man should exist; but he whose strongest passions are so conformable to the general interest, that he is almost constantly necessitated to be virtuous" (Helvétius, 1759: 289). The perceptive reader will see in this statement a striking similarity to the utopian ideas of communists of various persuasion.[23] Little wonder that he wrote extensively on the importance of education to achieve this end, and was thoroughly opposed to Rousseau's views, expressed in *Emile* that education should be designed to set men free from the chains into which they were born. This is not all that surprising, though from the point of view of Helvétius himself, it is ironic. He used this powerful idea of utility to demolish the practices and dogmas of the church. But his utilitarian system was so extreme, indeed, circular, since everything could be swallowed by it, the entire world could be seen only through its lens, which in the long run meant that he had replaced the religion of Catholicism with the religion of utilitarianism (Horowitz, 1954).

Third was his egalitarian zeal. The ideal of the equality of all was perhaps the one binding belief of all the *Philosophes* and other enlightenment thinkers of the period. But what each of them meant by "equality" varied strikingly among them. For example, Rousseau viewed equality as a condition that once existed in the innocent, primitive state of nature, before men began to think and do things that disturbed the order of nature. Technology provided progress, but the cost was inequality. On the contrary, Helvétius, along with Locke and Hume viewed human nature as completely fashioned by his later existence and position in social life. It was his social and economic relations (as Marx would say) that fashioned entirely his behavior whether alone or in groups, so it was the structure of society that should also be able to produce equality for all. Critics of Helvétius (Marx among them) argued that Helvétius managed to destroy the inequalities generated by religion, but made no indication how his utilitarian system would produce equality for all, in fact, one could see that, if men were different because of intelligence, physical attributes etc. it could produce more inequality, especially given that some men may be more adept at shoring up their own power. Helvétius solved this problem in two ways. First, he promoted the idea of the greatest happiness for the greatest number as did Beccaria, which leaves room for some who would be left out of the greatest happiness. Second, departing from the *Philosophes* and from Beccaria, he insisted that, since all were motivated by their own self love, as would be the sovereign, that one could not depend on the "wise ruler" or the "wise middle class" as the *Philosophes* variously advocated, but that the society should be democratic: all laws should be made in direct response to all individuals whose self interest was universally equal. It followed also that the role of the sovereign should be entirely utilitarian; the ruler should be merely the instrument of the masses.

Bentham

Bentham thought that Beccaria actually got his ideas from Helvétius: "... you who have raised your Italy so far above England, and I would add above France, were it not that Helvétius, without writing on the subject of laws, had already assisted you and provided you with your fundamental ideas...." (quoted in Maestro, 1973: 131).[24] But Bentham took Helvétius and transformed his ideas into a mechanistic, super utilitarian model. Indeed, Horowitz (1954) argues that Bentham transformed the utilitarianism of Helvétius that was driven by his belief in the natural rights of man, into a utilitarian capitalism, substituting the word "profit" for the word "pleasure." However, the relationship between utilitarianism and capitalism is very complex (as it is also for Marxism) though it could be said that both applications of utilitarianism held efficiency as their highest principle, each producing vastly different economies as a result. In any event, to the extent that Bentham shared the views of Beccaria, they had Helvétius in common.

Some have suggested that Bentham was a disciple of Beccaria because of his sentimental reference to Beccaria: "Oh, master, first evangelist of reason...." As H.L.A. Hart (1982) has shown, the relation between Bentham and Beccaria was complex. Bentham read Beccaria's *Treatise* when he was about nineteen, and probably wrote his *Rationale of Punishment* when he was about twenty nine. Hart argues, but admits it is speculative, that therefore Beccaria must have had a profound effect on

Bentham's young mind. He suggests even further that there are examples of Bentham's "unconscious borrowing" from Beccaria.[25]

However, Bentham was also critical of Beccaria on a number of points. Though he admired Beccaria's work because it was "based on reason" he also pointed out that "even in his work there is some reasoning drawn from false sources" (Bentham, 1975: 40). These false sources, one suspects, were the abstractions such as "natural rights" that were the cornerstone of the *Philosophes* and certainly popularized and promoted by Helvétius. Such abstractions as life, liberty, or property were meaningless unless specified exactly within the context of the utilitarian society, according to Bentham. If they could not be shown empirically to be useful to society, they were not rights. In fact, he was opposed to any idea that there were any rights that existed outside of, or beyond legal rights. Thus, he criticized Beccaria's failure to develop his general concepts in detail, to the point that Bentham thought Beccaria to be "rather a lazy man" (Hart, 1982: 49). But in Chapter VIII on the classification of crimes, Beccaria explicitly rejected the extensive classificatory systems as developed by Bentham:

> A systematic approach would now oblige us to examine and identify all the different sorts of crimes and how they should be punished. However, nature is so variable and circumstances change so much according to time and place that to do this would result in a work of immensely boring detail.

Boring indeed. Bentham developed extensive classificatory systems on just about everything, writing over five million words in his lifetime (Hart, 1982), a reason, perhaps, why few legislatures took any notice of his work, in spite of his constant nagging (see further below on the American Revolution).

On the other hand, Beccaria's promotion of the idea of the greatest happiness for the greater number" struck Bentham as much more "empirical" certainly less abstract, so that it could be simply defined by "counting heads," nevertheless effectively expressing the democratic ideal through Bentham's famous slogan: "Each [is] to count for one, and none for more than one." In the long run, this view boils down to the "contract with society" and the idea of direct democracy which was embraced by many of the social contract theorists, including Rousseau, as we saw earlier in this introduction. Finally, the most important thing they had in common was their emphasis on the major role that legislation should have in maximizing the happiness in society. This could be achieved through Bentham's theory of legal and other types of fictions, a theory that offered a complete alternative to English common law. But his theory was, ironically, too abstract and too far fetched to appeal to the legislators of England, whose legal system was dominated by common law, a hopelessly disorganized mess, according to Bentham. He had attended Blackstone's lectures (see below on the rule of law), and found them completely irrelevant to his own work. He preferred, as did the *Philosophes* to construct his own abstract theories. But it is probably to Bentham that England owes its tradition of utilitarian government, giving rise to the powerful middle class in England, especially the civil servants, who became the "technocrats" of the twentieth century.[26]

The Scots

Beirne (1993) has argued that the influence of the Scottish enlightenment on Beccaria has been greatly underestimated. The reason for this may be that the Scots as a definable group of enlightenment thinkers were not generally recognized as such until quite late in enlightenment scholarship, specifically when the Italian historian Franco Venturi argued in his address to the Eleventh Congress of the Historical Sciences in 1960, that they represented a distinct group that had labored more or less unknown in London. What bound them together, according to Venturi was their focus on the issue of progress in society (Venturi, 1960).[27] Beccaria most certainly reflects the influence of the Scottish enlightenment philosophers, especially Hutcheson (1725) and Hume, who thought of themselves as Newtonians, and revered the approach of Bacon. The Scots preferred a more inductive empirical approach, eschewing the invention of abstract ideas of progress adhered to by the *Philosophes*, pointing out that such ideas had little relation to the facts of history (Hume's view of course). To this extent theirs was a more down to earth view of science, man and society. Of considerable interest also was their view, especially by Hume, that the senses were the source of all knowledge, not reason. This contrasted greatly with the *Philosophes* since they were, generally, thinkers first, and observers second, that is to say their approach was deductive, as exemplified by Montesquieu.

The Scots, in contrast were inductive. They began with observation, and this meant, generally, they began with nature. There, one could find order, beauty and thus morality. History was a series of events ordained by nature and Hume applied this view in his classic *History of England*. It was a "natural history" which, if examined objectively was the source of truth. This truth, as we saw earlier, was used by Hume to demolish the idea of the social contract. Finally, in nature lay a mathematical symmetry. All these views came together to promote an especially economic and down to earth approach to explaining man and society. The solid basis for it was established by Hutcheson (1755), whose influence seeped into Beccaria's penchant for economic and mathematical analysis at places throughout the *Treatise*. Hutcheson was also critical of Hobbes's negative view of human nature, preferring instead to argue that man, naturally sociable, was motivated by "enlightened self interest," a motivational theory that later formed the backbone of Adam Smith's *The Wealth of Nations*. Beccaria, critical of Hobbes in his introductory chapters, seems to affirm Hutcheson's view, but whether this is Hutcheson's view as against a similar, though very romantic view of the innate goodness of human nature as promoted by Rousseau is an open question. Furthermore, Beccaria, as we have already observed was clearly ambivalent. While in "To the Reader," he explains the original wolf like nature of man as a "corruption" of his true nature, ("...the state of nature that preceded society was born by the corruption of human nature and lack of a clear direction from above..") later and sprinkled throughout the *Treatise* he clearly assumes that, if it were not for law (based on the social contract) all hell would break loose, such as "... understanding that this is necessary to keep the internal ferment and selfishness of human nature under control" (Chapter IV).

Common Misunderstandings of the *Treatise*

A "classic" invariably becomes a book that is often quoted or paraphrased by those who have not read it—or quite possibly think they have read it because it is so widely known. A book to which is attributed an entire reform movement in penology and criminal justice therefore often has ascribed to it many of the values and arguments of reformers, even though they may not in fact be present. This fact, plus Beccaria's equivocation and obscurity on many issues has given rise to a number of mistaken or questionable interpretations of the *Treatise*. In what follows we review some of the major misunderstandings.

Torture

Beccaria achieved much of his fame because of his opposition to torture:

> But I would add that the ultimate confusion arises when a tortured man becomes both accuser and accused at the same time; when pain becomes the crucible of truth, as though it resides in the very muscles and nerves of his miserable body. This is a sure method to absolve the robust wicked and condemn the innocent weak (Chapter XVI).

While some have criticized Beccaria's definition or use of the concept of torture, here we agree with his definition.[28] That is, torture is the use of physical and mental pain in order to extract information, usually confessions or identification of collaborators which means that it confounds the punishment with the process of finding guilt. In contrast, corporal punishment, which is often confused with torture, is simply the application of physical pain after, and separate from, the finding of guilt and pronouncement of sentence (Newman, 1983). One aspect of torture is very apparent and reveals a difficulty with the utilitarian approach to punishment: torture is above all a means end process, it is utilitarian to the core. It is understandable, therefore, that Beccaria was actually ambiguous on the use of torture. Although he rails against the use of pain to obtain confessions and to accuse collaborators, we find in the section "Suggestive Interrogations, Depositions" of the *Treatise* a statement that directly contradicts this view:

> One who is interrogated and refuses to respond to questioning deserves a punishment fixed by law, and a punishment of the severest kind (Chapter XXXVIII).

According to Beccaria's own definition of torture, this statement actually advocates it. That the "punishment be fixed by law" does not change it from being torture. The punishments used in the tortures (that is, the physical punishments and the procedures for administering them) of the Holy Inquisition were carefully spelled out and very specific according to Canon Law. The mere fact that the punishments are legislated does not rule out the use of torture. In fact strictly speaking his advocacy of "punishment" is not punishment at all, since punishments can only be applied after the finding of guilt. Beccaria here either intentionally or mistakenly confuses punishment with torture.

Finally, Beccaria's proposal of perpetual slavery (as we shall see below) appears to be consistent with this harsh utilitarian approach. This may be regarded as an especially cruel form of punishment which allows for complete control over the entire life and bodies of the condemned persons for an extended period of time. This is not torture, per se, since it has no specific utilitarian aim, like obtaining a confession. But it is an excessively drawn out form of corporal and mental punishment. It may not technically be torture, but it surely is.[29]

The Death Penalty

More than his views on torture, Beccaria is revered for his "absolute" opposition to the death penalty. Indeed, his biographers say, this position was even more extreme than those of other reformers of the time, such as Voltaire and Montesquieu. Beccaria's famous argument against the death penalty was that the sentence of slavery was more severe and therefore a greater deterrent than death. We question him on several counts.

First, penal slavery was a devious way of inflicting death. Sellin (1976: 66) has described Beccaria's argument against the death penalty as "specious." The conditions made it quite likely that the offender would die. This was especially so when time was served in ships' galleys. In fact, galley slavery was considered appropriate for a "capital offense." It is not clear, therefore, how "absolute" Beccaria's opposition to the death penalty was, since many would die as a result of the punishments he proposed, and they would die in a long drawn out process of suffering.

Second, his argument that penal slavery was a greater deterrent than death is questionable (Sellin, 1976: 66). Because of the extremely painful ways that death was inflicted during his time, it is difficult to see how the punishment of penal slavery would be any *more* deterrent. He is thus led to advocate horrible punishments in order to demonstrate the deterrent value of slavery. He notes: "It is not the intensity of punishment that has the greatest effect on the human mind, but its duration..." (Chapter XXVIII). Brutality in the name of deterrence is clearly advocated by Beccaria when he approvingly notes, "... between fetters and chains, under the rod, under the yoke, or in an iron cage...the desperate criminal does not end his suffering, but just begins it" (Chapter XXVIII). And he concludes that, "This is the advantage of the punishment of slavery, which frightens those who see it more than those who suffer it, for the former see the total of all the unhappy moments, and the latter suffer the unhappiness of a single moment in the here and now, with no mind to the future" (Chapter XXVIII).

His arguments here deeply contradict his claims to advocate mild punishments as we will see shortly. In fact, he had argued in other parts of the *Treatise* that harsh punishments worked *against* deterrence. His only response to this criticism could be that penal slavery was *less* harsh than death as then inflicted.

Beccaria made two other arguments against the death penalty that are popular today. First, that the death penalty is irrevocable. However the alternative he advocates, penal slavery for life, cannot be revoked either, unless there is a way to turn back the clock. Obviously one could apply the same criticism to his advocacy of corporal punishments (see below). Second, he claimed that execution was a form of "legalized murder." If this is so, logically penal slavery must be regarded as "legalized kidnapping." He later added another argument when serving on the commission for the Lombard code in 1791. This was that "absolute proofs sufficient for sentencing a man to death do not exist ... not even the confession of the accused..." (Maestro, 1973: 144-150). He was strongly criticized by other members of the commission for this extreme stand. Though on this, he was probably right.

Mildness of Punishments?

It appears that Beccaria did not advocate mild punishments at all. Clearly, he did not advocate them in his argument against the death penalty. Furthermore, he advocates corporal punishments for some crimes. Is it consistent for an enlightened reformer of his time to advocate corporal punishment? Section XXVI of the *Treatise* clearly advocates just this:

> Some crimes are committed against the person, others against property. The former must be unerringly punished with corporal punishment (Chapter XX).

Beccaria fails to specify what corporal punishments he approves. Does one assume that he had no criticism of the current practices (e.g. , whipping, breaking on the wheel, removing bodily parts with red-hot pincers etc.)? Instead this section moves on to an advocacy of equal punishments for both the nobleman and the "least citizen." This is a clever ruse: corporal punishments for violent crimes, but let's have equality for all.[30]

The Classical School and Judicial Discretion

Beccaria has been described as the founder of the "classical school" of criminology[31]. This school is usually characterized as one that is "administrative" (Vold and Bernard, 1986) in its approach, and this is contrasted in many textbooks with the "scientific" or "positive school" which developed under the leadership of Lombroso and later Ferri in Italy. Beccaria's "administrative" criminology is seen as rooted in his critique of judicial discretion. He was persistent in his denunciation of judicial discretion, using scientific principles of objectivity to reveal their abusive practices. This was probably done without much experience of how actually the criminal justice system operated. Paolucci (1963) argues that Beccaria knew very little of courts and judges, and that his claim that many of the problems of the criminal justice process were caused by the abuse of judicial discretion was simply unfounded.

In any event, Beccaria's solution to the discretion problem was to enact very specific laws and thus abolish judicial discretion completely. Modern experts on sentencing have observed that all this does is shift the discretion from one level to another, in this case the legislative body. One can see that this "reform" is hardly a reform. It instead leads to the concentration of power in the hands of the sovereign. Or, if the State is ruled more by the legislative body (such as in England, and after the Revolution in France) the laws become unwieldy and inflexible, since they must account for an incredible amount of detail, and this must be acted upon by a political body (the legislatures) which are renowned for having difficulty in reaching decisions. In fact, the 1795 Code of Misdemeanors and Punishments enacted in France in the third Brumaire, year IV (October 25, 1795) fixed specific and unalterable punishments giving the judge not the slightest choice. This code proved unworkable, since it was impossible for any code to foresee the wide range of circumstances that might occur in each case. This inflexibility was eventually removed with the revisions brought about by the Napoleonic Codes (Maestro, 1942: 140-147).

Utilitarian or Retributivist?

The definitional problems in distinguishing between retributivism and utilitarianism make for much confusion in understanding Beccaria's position. Young (1983: 10) argues that Beccaria is essentially a retributivist and only secondarily a utilitarian. He reaches this conclusion largely as a result of defining retribution very broadly, and by more or less taking anything that Kant and Hegel said about punishment as definitional of retribution. However, the supreme role of the sovereign or State that both Hegel and Kant allowed in the role of punishment is not an essential element of retribution (Newman, 2008: 193).

Young (1983) also claims that assessing seriousness of crimes only by their consequences, which Beccaria does, is commensurate with retributivism. One type of retributivism may be in line with this view, ("secular retribution") if it is used as a simple matching formula to connect a particular crime with a particular punishment (Newman, 1983). However, in general, the consequentialist structure of this model makes it a very doubtful element of retributive logic. Barbara Wooton (1959), perhaps the strongest twentieth century advocate of utilitarian criminal justice, has used injury and damage of the crime as the main element in her utilitarian theory of punishment. By far the dominant ethic of retribution historically has been to require individual guilt (i.e., evil intent) of the actor, in order to (1) justify punishing the actor in the first place— the offender must be shown to have consciously intended the act, and (2) match the punishment to the offender's guilt ("religious retribution," see: Newman, 2008). For retributivists, the damage done by the act is important, but secondary, though they are also insistent that "rules are rules" and must be obeyed because they are rules, and that probably the worst damage of the act is that the rule was broken. But one can see that obedience to rules is very much a utilitarian idea that is embedded in Beccaria's approach, since without obedience (by way of any version of the social contract) society would dissolve. This is therefore utilitarian at its core, not retributive.[32]

Beccaria's, utilitarian assumptions are particularly interesting because they appear to contradict some of his other "administrative" postulates. We can see these in his famous concluding sentence that has captivated generations of readers:

> ... we can construct a general theory of great utility ... So that every punishment should not be an act of violence of one or many against a private citizen, it must be essentially public, prompt, necessary, the minimum possible in the given circumstances, proportionate to the crimes, and dictated by the laws.

Retributivists would certainly agree that a punishment should be proportionate to the crime; that is their credo—some would say their only credo. However, it is contradicted by the utilitarian view that the pain of the punishment must outweigh the pleasure of the offense. This is in fact what is hidden by Beccaria's use of the words "least possible" and "necessary." What is the necessary condition for punishment—the breaking of a law? Retributivists would say so. But utilitarians, who are forward looking, are interested in preventing future crimes. This is why they have long advocated increasing punishments for second and subsequent offenses, and why they advocate punishment by example—general deterrence (the reason for Beccaria's insistence of the punishment being public).

These punishment policies directly contradict the idea of proportionate punishments. Rather, their thrust is towards applying punishment that is *greater* than the crime. In other words disproportionate punishments. Indeed, Beccaria notes in his chapter on "The Mildness of Punishments,"

> "... punishment obtains sufficient effect when its severity just exceeds the benefit the offender receives from the crime, and the degree of excess must be calculated precisely according to the damage to public good caused by the crime" (Chapter XXVII).

There is nothing whatsoever in these utilitarian views that guarantees mildness of punishments. On the contrary, the utilitarian principles guarantee an increasingly severe punishment.

In sum, we see clearly that Beccaria incorporated the retributive justification for punishment into a utilitarian model. This served to sanitize the less appealing deterrent assumptions of the utilitarian position he advocated. That is, by advocating "proportionate" punishment, he was able to make his position seem just. But it is clear that he did not have in mind the kind of "just deserts" advocated by modern day retributivists (Newman, 2008).

Legacy of the *Treatise*[33]

As we know, the book was an instant success, widely acclaimed as the bible for reform of the criminal justice system, especially penology (Newman and Marongiu, 1990). Yet it is clear that its contents, ambiguity, equivocation, shaky logic, and superficiality do not substantively warrant the term "classic." At least, not a scholarly classic. Some have argued, however, that its simplicity is unfairly characterized as superficial. That its clarity in stating what reforms are needed and what was wrong with the criminal justice system are what make it a classic reformist tract. Beccaria may not have had any idea about the contemporary criminal justice system, and this did not matter. The force with which he stated his reformist ideas is what counted. And certainly there is some support to this view, since, interspersed among his many obscurities there are some sparkling clear and even poetic sentences that convey the ideals of the enlightenment. Certainly, the final paragraph of the book is an eloquent, resplendent, concise statement that sums up the entire book.

There is little doubt that Beccaria's ideas were used and promulgated by many other reformers at the time. His phrase "greatest happiness for the greater number" found its way into many essays. Jeremy Bentham probably made that statement famous. The *Treatise* was widely promulgated, and used by the great reformers. In that sense it had an enormous effect. Jenkins (1984) explains its popularity in the eighteenth century simply by the fact that the reforms advocated by Beccaria were already in the process of emerging as part of the overall spirit of enlightenment of the eighteenth century. Those sovereigns who quickly embraced his *Treatise* had already shown their inclination towards reform. These included the Empress Catherine II of Russia, The Grand Duke Leopold of Tuscany and Frederick II of Prussia. However, the major policy advocated by Beccaria—removal of discretion from judges—actually led to placing greater power in the hands of the State as we noted earlier. That the resulting Napoleonic Codes represented a definite "break with the horrors of the past," as Maestro (1972) says, there can be no doubt. But it is another thing to claim that it was Beccaria and his *Treatise* that were responsible for this break. The French Revolution, after all, came about as a result of many complex historical conditions. It was this revolution that produced the situation in which Beccaria's policies could be applied. One could say that Beccaria wrote the right thing at the right time.[34]

The Rule of Law

It may be surprising to our readers that we did not include the idea of the "rule of law" as one of Beccaria's master themes, since the idea is often attributed to him and other enlightenment thinkers (Bierne, 1991: 778; Caso, 1975). However, the idea gained popularity only in the latter half of the twentieth century when economically developed nations began to turn to "doing good" among those nations that were not prospering. These "undeveloped" nations as they were termed by the United Nations Development Program became recipients of large amounts of economic aid which often returned few discernible benefits to the people of those countries. Towards the end of the twentieth century it became a mantra that economic aid was relatively wasted if the rule of law was not first established.

Generally, the idea of the rule of law, as inferred by Beccaria's interpreters is that we should have a government of laws, not of men. This is the clear intent of Beccaria's thorough and absolute denunciation of judicial discretion, which in turn is the logical application of the "science of man" master theme that demands objectivity and impartiality in all maters of political life. That judges would have no discretion would seem to suggest that they would have no opportunity to display impartiality, which leads to the second problem with Beccaria's understanding of the rule of law: it places a great deal of reliance on the efficiency of a system of laws of substance and procedures which means that, without the input of human judgment, that system must be infallible. This, of course, is an impossibility and remains a hidden affirmation by Beccaria of the wisdom of law as a body unto itself. It is acclaimed by Caso (1975) as a wonderful insight, when he uses Thomas Paine's (1776) famous observation to praise Beccaria:

> "... LAW IS KING. For as in absolute governments the king is law, so in free countries the law ought to be King; and there ought to be no other."

A moment's reflection on this famous characterization of the rule of law is enough to reveal that there are also bad kings, so there may also be bad laws, which could be a disastrous situation in a system where humans cannot intervene to soften the effects of bad law.[35] So to have a rule of law is not enough, which Beccaria of course understood; it is why the social contract forms the essential core of his *Treatise*. The law must be in some way held accountable to the people against whom it is administered. But we are also led by this line of argument to understand that the administration of the law must also be made part of the "rule of law." In Chapter XIII on witnesses, Beccaria advises "the rule of law demands that one is innocent until proved guilty." He continues in this chapter to advocate what seems to be an adversary system of criminal justice in which a prosecutor's role is separated from the judge. This was (and is) contrary to the inquisitorial system where an investigative judge also acts as a prosecutor and accumulates the evidence. The latter system still holds sway in most European countries, although it is gradually being chipped away. Certainly, the proponents of the adversarial system (dominant in the United States and other Anglo-Saxon countries) claim that this is the only sure way to eliminate the temptations of judicial bias in presuming guilt as they make their investigation. The prosecutor may also presume guilt, but he must also prove it to the judge in court, and most likely a jury as well. But in other places, Beccaria does not carefully distinguish between judge and prosecutor, using the general terms *magistrato* or *giudice* to refer to either. Neither judge nor prosecutor are mentioned in Chapter XXX on Criminal Proceedings, nor in Chapter XXXVIII on Suggestive Interrogations. Indeed, in the latter case he seems to open the door to the use of torture against those who refuse to answer questions during an interrogation. It is never stated who would in fact administer such measures. Beccaria tirelessly distinguishes judges from legislators, but nowhere does he clearly distinguish them from the administrators of the law.

Finally, the derivation of the idea of the rule of law is very much an abstract notion in Beccaria's hands, much as it was in the hands of other enlightenment thinkers, particularly the *Philosophes*. Its foundation rests essentially on the idea of natural law as we have described it earlier in this introduction. However, there is quite another way to view the origins of the rule of law, and that is one that follows Hume's historical approach. Such an approach would take seriously the body of common law produced in the English common law system as an accumulation of legal wisdom (which the enlightenment thinkers were anxious to discard as products of religion and privilege). The wisdom of the ages might conceivably be construed as a bit like natural law, but it does not bring with it the weighty philosophical and religious baggage of natural law. The great English masters of common law, particularly Blackstone (1765) are never so much as mentioned by Beccaria and rarely by other enlightenment thinkers of Europe (and constantly derided by Bentham). There may be several reasons for this, perhaps the main one being that there was and continues to be a strong tradition favoring common law over legal codes as the best way to preserve or promulgate the "rule of law." Because of his disdain for judges, Beccaria put all his eggs in the basket of legislation. And at the time of his writing, the English common law had been exported to America where law was not viewed as king, but rather as the king's law; a condition ripe for Beccaria's ideas.

The American Revolution

There is little doubt that the ideas of the enlightenment thinkers, especially the *Philosophes* and probably Beccaria, had considerable influence on the founding fathers at least up to the Declaration of Independence. Consider the following passage from the second paragraph of the Declaration, a passage used to justify the revolution:

> WE hold these Truths to be self-evident, that all Men are created equal, that they are endowed by their Creator with certain inalienable Rights, that among these are Life, Liberty, and the Pursuit of Happiness—That to secure these Rights, Governments are instituted among Men, deriving their just Powers from the Consent of the Governed.

The "inalienable rights" flow directly from natural law, "life" from the right of survival first identified by Hobbes, "liberty" the key term in all of social contract theory justifying government, and the all embracing "pursuit of happiness" expressed by Beccaria in his expression "the greatest happiness for the greater number."[36] Though we are not certain that Beccaria was the first to use this expression in his writing, the style is very close to the occasional flashes of eloquence we find in the *Treatise*. But we also find this style in Montesquieu and Voltaire.

However, there are two other reasons that suggest that it is very likely that Beccaria's *Treatise* did directly influence the founding fathers. First is the level of generality and style with which it was written. We have criticized Beccaria for his vagueness and superficiality in many places of the *Treatise*. But in one important way this was its strength, since it could easily be adapted and reproduced in the "war of pamphlets" that continued in the colonies throughout the 1760s well past the signing of the Constitution. These pamphlets contained much that was inflammatory, even defamatory. Loyalists and Patriots[37] cited Beccaria constantly, as was also the case back in London where both Whigs and Tories quoted him with approval (Bailyn, 1967). People complained, just as they do today, that the Pamphlets recognized no limits and purveyed the most vile and crass information aimed to titillate and anger their readers, so much so that their circulation would be extended as far and wide as possible. The parallels with the modern day radio and television talk shows are quite striking. Important people complained that the very core of their culture was being undermined by these irreverent and coarse pamphlets. Yet of great interest is that almost all of these pamphlets drew on many of the sources we have covered in the beginning of this Introduction—the works of the classical scholars, especially those of Rome, that lay behind the ideas of social contract and natural law, especially the ideas of classical Roman law, society and dialogues[38]; all of these distorted and popularized, even though the majority of educated citizens would have been well acquainted with their works (Gummere, 1963). The most effective Pamphleteer was Thomas Paine, a great admirer of Beccaria (Caso, 1975) who popularized the idea, as we saw earlier, that "LAW IS KING."

The second reason why it is very likely that Beccaria's ideas influenced the founding fathers was that at least two of them were known to have read the *Treatise*, both of them lawyers, both of whom quoted Beccaria during the course of their professions. John Adams made notes of adoration in his diary and used a most famous passage in his unpopular case in which he successfully defended Captain Preston and his soldiers in charges resulting from the Boston Massacre in 1770. He supposedly electrified the jury when he quoted an extract from Beccaria that he had previously entered into his diary:

"If, by supporting the Rights of Mankind, and of invincible Truth, I shall contribute to save from the Agonies of Death one unfortunate Victim of Tyranny, or of Ignorance, equally fatal; his Blessing and Tears of Transport, will be sufficient Consolation to me, for the Contempt of all Mankind" (Adams, 1770 [1961]).[39]

Adams was known to have purchased an Italian edition of the *Treatise* as early as 1768 and may have tried to translate it, since there is a record of his having paid for Italian lessons and an entry in his diary in Italian which reads: " *Le pene che oltrepassano la necessità di conservare il deposito della Salute publica, sono ingiuste di lor natura*" which may have been a translation from his own English which was written before it as: "Every Act of Authority, of one Man over another for which there is not an absolute Necessity, is tyrannical" (Caso, 1975: 17). Though it is possible that Adams used a different Italian edition from ours, we could find just one sentence that was slightly similar to this in the penultimate sentence of Chapter II, The Right to Punish: "... *tutte le pene che oltrepassano la necessità di conservare questo vincolo sono ingiuste di lor natura*" which we translate as "... all punishments that go beyond what is necessary to conserve this bond [of individuals to society] are inherently unjust." Adams's pronouncement is much more eloquent.

Jefferson had at least twenty six extracts from the *Treatise* in his *Commonplace Book* (Chinard, 1926: 314; see also Bailyn, 1967: Caso, 1975; Kimball, 1943). It is popularly believed that Jefferson, in coining the wording of the opening passage quoted above from the Declaration of Independence originally wrote "Life, Liberty, and Property" but later changed it to Life, Liberty and the Pursuit of Happiness." Whether this is true or not, and if true, whether it can be attributed specifically to Beccaria's influence can never be known with certainty. However, we have noted in a number of places that Beccaria was certainly ambivalent about the role of property, so its inclusion in the declaration would probably not have been an indication of Beccaria's influence.

The extent to which Beccaria might have influenced the American Constitution is much more difficult to determine. The separation of powers is perhaps the most conspicuous example of enlightenment thinkers, but as we have seen, Beccaria did not adopt this as completely in his writing as did Montesquieu and perhaps also Locke. The important, indeed preeminent role of law and its legislation does have a major part in Beccaria's *Treatise*, and certainly it is supreme in the U.S. Constitution. The Constitution pointedly begins with the legislative powers and their administration of Article I. Judicial powers come later in Article III. Beccaria would have been proud. However, Beccaria's influence, if any, is more pronounced in the long list of complaints in the Declaration of Independence that are leveled against the "Present King of Great Britain." The first three are specifically concerned with good and bad laws about which Beccaria had much to say (Chapters XL and XLI), and the majority of the others (some twenty-seven complaints) are concerned with the King's failure to support proper legislation that was relevant to specific conditions of the far flung colonies.

In sum, Beccaria probably had a vague, general influence on thinking that went into the Declaration of Independence, possibly found their way into the Constitution, and maybe the slogans that were used to maintain the necessary fervor in opposing the British tyranny (Lundberg and May, 1976; Lutz, 1984). But all of the above should be tempered by the empirical scholarship of the twentieth century. About one-third of all libraries in the period 1777–90 contained a copy of the *Treatise* (Lundberg and May, 1976) and Lutz (1984) found that Beccaria accounted for about 1% of citations in the 1770s, 3% in the 1780s and 0% in the 1790s. These findings are rather salutary, but not fatal to those who would champion Beccaria's legacy.

The "Spirit" of Beccaria

Some commentators on Beccaria who are aware of the weaknesses in logic of the *Treatise* have argued that it is not the logic that is so important, but rather its "heart." By using this more general interpretation of Beccaria, they are able to point to its "liberating" influence on almost every criminal code in the world that they identify as "enlightened." There is no mistaking that those who would characterize themselves as "liberal" in their views of criminal justice seem to embrace Beccaria's general spirit of reform.

Liberals embrace Beccaria's general position that favors milder punishments along with the utilitarian assumption that the infliction of pain and suffering on criminals is evil-in-itself. This spirit has continued through to the present with the strong movement towards the rehabilitation of offenders and the still pervasive treatment model in penology, though supplanted to some extent by restorative justice. The treatment model, though under fierce attack, nevertheless still dominates the language of penology. Colleges still teach courses called "corrections," rarely courses on "punishment." What is it about this spirit of liberalism that makes it endure so?

Part of the answer lies within utilitarian philosophy itself. It rests on a profound contradiction. On the one hand, the utilitarians from Beccaria to Bentham advocate the least possible punishment. Yet at the same time they advocate an all pervasive deterrent approach, such that it requires massive intervention by the state to enforce such a program. While they give lip service to the old utilitarian ethic of the social contract (one gives up only a small portion of one's self interest to the state so that all may pursue their individual interests) they advocate policies which require the state to become larger and larger. We saw in our review of the social contract theorists that they foundered—understandably—on this very problem. That the utilitarians of the eighteenth century should have promoted a policy that directly enhanced the power of the state is puzzling, given that the evidence for abuse of power by the state was all round them, and certainly one of the factors that led to the French Revolution, and the social unrest that occurred in England. It was, perhaps, only Hume, the historian, who saw and understood this problem.

It is within this framework that we should see the transformation of criminal justice, especially penology, that occurred in relation to Beccaria and the other utilitarians. The popular belief is that milder punishments resulted from their reforms. By what measure do we conclude that punishments are milder today that in Beccaria's time? It would seem that the product of the eighteenth-century reforms was prison, a solution to crime that has spread like an infectious disease. Is this punishment milder than the several corporal punishments applied in the eighteenth century? Is the proportion of punishments to crimes demonstrably more just? If we take the massive prison terms that are dealt out for non-violent crimes in most states of the United States and other countries, one must remain skeptical. And the actual specific pains that occur in prison are rarely taken seriously (Newman, 1983), just as Beccaria did not take seriously the pains of slavery as a punishment in his argument against the death penalty.

It is true that we no longer have the aggravated forms of the death penalty in this century (that is, various slow and bloody ways of inflicting death, such as drawing and quartering)—though the aggravation is of a different, and mental, kind given the delays in carrying out a death sentence that are typical of this punishment today. At the time Beccaria wrote, punishment of the body was in the process of being replaced with control of the body as so well demonstrated by Foucault (1977). The reasons for this transformation are complex, but one identified by Foucault was the need in a rapidly growing industrial society for disciplined workers. Foucault manages to draw together the growth of the organized society—through education, the military and later the factory —to produce a disciplined work force. The byproduct of this drastic transformation of society was to focus punishment away from the body and onto controlling the lives of the accused. Penal slavery and prison were natural consequences of this ethos. Thus, it can be seen that there were massive historical changes underway that created a climate in which Beccaria's reforms could flourish. His opposition to the death penalty and advocacy of penal slavery and prison were exactly in step. His plea for "mildness of punishments" suited perfectly the transformation from bodily punishments to those that manipulated or controlled the person. The utilitarian ethos—control—was served admirably by Beccaria's strong advocacy of deterrence. Paradoxically, it is crime control that is also the mantra of modern day conservatives.

Notes

1. We use the generic male gender expression throughout this Introduction and the Note to the Text that follows to reflect accurately the writing style of the eighteenth-century thinkers.
2. There are differing views concerning the relationship between nature as physical phenomena and natural law as a human phenomenon. Passerin D' Entrèves (1994),

for example denies that natural law has anything to do with physical nature and is entirely and distinctively human.

3. Hobbes is often misinterpreted as depicting individuals as pursuing their own interests regardless of others'. However, he conceived of individual interests very narrowly, in terms of basic survival. This did not, for example, include the pursuit of private property which he saw as a creation of government, not as a part of nature, as had, for example Grotius, as we noted earlier.

4. The idea of a primitive state of nature was widespread among eighteenth century enlightenment thinkers, but there was much confusion over what exactly was the primitive state of nature, based largely on a romantic view of primitive peoples, which would later become a preoccupation in the nineteenth century when knowledge of primitive tribes in distant lands became more common. The general notion though, that chaos and disorder would result if humans were left to their own devices without the controls of civil society, remains to this day a powerful idea among theorists (many relying of Freudian ideas of innate aggressive instincts) and criminal justice practitioners (Campbell et al., 1970).

5. If this has an uncanny Marxist ring to it, there is no puzzle here. Much of early Marxist theory was devoted to the eradication of the State (including private property which Hobbes saw as created by government), so that civil society could emerge to free individuals from all the chains that Rousseau railed against.

6. Beccaria adopts this view in his "To the Reader," and in other places where he observes that the innate goodness of human nature has been corrupted by the errors of society ("…Very few have thought to return to basic principles in order to eradicate the accumulated errors of many centuries, or at least to use the persuasiveness that only acknowledged truth can provide to curb the rampant course of misguided power…") (Introduction). By "acknowledged truth" it is likely that he means "natural law."

7. This is an argument, it may be noted, of expediency, an issue debated among natural law proponents and critics, the point being that one cannot equate expediency with justice.

8. This view presages the works of late nineteenth century thinkers such as Kropotkin (1972) who argued that, far from being innately aggressive, man was, along with most species, disposed towards helping and cooperating with others of his species. Recent works by neo-Darwinians make similar claims, based on the idea of reciprocity (Cosmides and Tooby, 1989; Gottschalk, 2002), though they also recognize the important role of aggression and competition. Thus, the social contract according to this view is no big deal, not an inevitable result of men's needing to protect themselves, but rather a natural outcome of human nature (not driven by anything except reproduction of DNA). The neo Darwinian view solves the problem that many critics of the social contract highlighted, which is that no one at any point in time can be shown to have actually consciously chosen to enter into any social contract with either the state or society. The Darwinian view is that these "agreements" evolved through natural selection over many millions of generations as a result of individual organisms reciprocating with others, so that societies of patterned reciprocity emerged which increased the survival chances of the individual organisms living in that society. Ants, after all, work incredibly well together. Their society works well not because of the individual choices made by each ant. It just works.

9. It is worth considering, however, that the ready solution was offered by Adam Smith's theory of markets driven by self interest that created overall wealth in an economy, so that all eventually benefited by the pursuit of private property. His

theory can also be seen as a logical extension of natural law theory. Obviously Marx, among others, would never agree!

10.   This reveals Locke's idea of the original state of nature. Rousseau, we saw, wanted to think of it as a "positive" community—where individuals would act positively with the good of all in mind, a good of greater value than each individual good. Other natural law theorists had also developed this idea, though with difficulty. For example, Sir Robert Filmer (Laslett, 1949) who distinguished between "negative" and "positive" communities in his critique of Locke, which some would say was misguided (Buckle 1991: 162-166). Here, Locke clearly assumes a "negative" community, that requires regulation to maintain harmony.

11.   Though Hobbes did in fact reserve the right for the people to overthrow the sovereign if it turned out that it was not doing its job of protecting them.

12.   Lest this position seem too outrageous to the reader of the twenty-first century, we should pause to consider the critics of the U.S. invasion of Iraq who appear to argue that the previous government, no matter how bad, was better than none, or perhaps, better than half a government. Hume is well supported by this historical event—where was the consent of the governed? Did the referendum conducted in 2003 truly reveal the consent of the governed? Hume would have said, "not a chance."

13.   Curiously, at the same time as Beccaria, another Italian laboring in obscurity in an insignificant position at the University of Naples, Giambattista Vico (1725), outlined what he called "The New Science." It contained most or all of the ideas put forward not only by Beccaria, but Montesquieu and others who came later than Vico. It seems that his *New Science* was possibly purchased by Montesquieu, but not read (Adams, 1935; Hazard, 1954: 37). Vico's brilliance in always giving obeisance to religion, but at the same time embracing Francis Bacon, especially the inductive method, could have established a model for Beccaria to follow. Nowhere does Beccaria acknowledge him, although Caso (1975: 246) claims that Beccaria derived many of his ideas from Vico.

14.   Smith had observed: "… a quiet commercial rivalry among nations has arisen, a healthy competition worthy of rational men." Beccaria (1766) even published a paper that advocated an economic analysis and solution to smuggling.

15.   Quite a few of Beccaria's other (less distinguished) writings were on economics. This passage has an almost modern ring to it, presaging Adam Smith's *Inquiry into the Wealth of Nations*, published just twelve years after the *Treatise*, in which Smith argues that the free pursuit of individual self interest through open markets and competition is a major builder of wealth (read happiness) for all (Smith, 1976). Smith was an active member of the Scottish enlightenment thinkers, which included Hutcheson, one of his teachers, Hume and Locke all of whom have influenced Beccaria's writings to some degree.

16.   Francioni 1984: 23, fn 2 in fact notes that the original formula comes from Francis Hutcheson (1726: III, 177-78)

17.   The definition of punishment is neither obvious nor simple. See Newman (1983, 2008)

18.   We choose Freud as the twentieth century example of this approach, but the importance of the proximity both in time and place between a forbidden act and its punishment was taken much further in the fields of classical and operant conditioning during the first half of that century. See Newman (2008).

19.   Turgot was an economist who wrote, among other works, *On the Historical Progress of the Human Mind*.

20.   Condorcet also addressed from a statistical point of view the problem of how majority decisions were made—a problem as we noted above that lies beneath

the "greatest happiness" principle. This became known as Condorcet's paradox from his 1785 *Essay on the Application of Analysis to the Probability of Majority Decisions.*

21. Though one can find, predictably, the opposite point of view in Rousseau and to some extent in Locke, that the "spirit" or "general will" remains constant and provides the continuity of history. From this idea developed an entirely different view of "progress" very much of the Hegelian variety and generally the German philosophical tradition.

22. For reviews of the "persecution" and "martyrdom" of Helvétius see: Smith (1965). Helvétius was harshly criticized, even made fun of, for recanting his *De L'esprit* (Wootton, 2000).

23. In fact, Helvétius formed an important basis for much of Marx and Engels in the development of Marxist theory. See for example Horowitz (1954) who effectively demonstrates the importance of Helvétius to the development of Marxist and neo Marxist thought.

24. In fact some consider that it was the work of Helvétius that spawned the *Treatise* though Beccaria never publicly acknowledged it (Wootton, 2000).

25. Hart argues, for example, that Bentham's theory of logical fictions—which probably spawned the entire field of semiotics—may have been stimulated by a minor footnote by Beccaria to Chapter III, on the meaning of the word "obligation."

26. The utilitarian approach to government was advocated and implemented by Bentham's ardent supporter James Mill who became a powerful civil servant in his own right, and later by his son John Stuart Mill (1891) and many after him.

27. It should be added, however, that although they were a distinct group in terms of their interests, there was considerable dissension among them. See Robertson (2008).

28. Paolucci (1963: 31) an unfriendly translator of the *Treatise* criticized Beccaria for equating torture with trials by ordeal. As he notes, this followed closely the work of the Verris on torture. But Beccaria was right to focus on torture as an integral part of the guilt finding process. Trials by ordeal are somewhat similar, though not the same. Paolucci claims that Beccaria's criticism of torture "was a desperate abuse of the rationalistic desire to secure the 'consent of the governed'. "This hardly detracts from Beccaria's argument. Paolucci fails to comprehend the distinction between corporal punishment and torture. See Newman (1983).

29. For a more extensive account of the problem of torture in Beccaria's time, see: Verri (1988). This is the basic work used by Alesssandro Manzoni (Beccaria's grandson) in his well known book, *Storia della colonna infame.* ("The Story of the Column of Infamy"), a report of the same judicial enquiry described by Verri, which took place in Milan in summer 1630 during a virulent plague. It refers to the case of the anointers (*untori*) who were suspected of spraying the walls of the city with infected liquids in order to spread infection. On the basis of mere suspicion, two innocent men, Guglielmo Piazza, a Commissioner of the Tribunal of Health and Gian Giacomo Mora, a barber, were arrested and, after a confession extorted with torture and false promises of impunity, were executed by breaking on the wheel. Mora`s house was razed, and a column, called the Column of Infamy, was erected there in memory of this event. Manzoni published in 1840 *La storia della colonna infame*, along with the revised edition of I *promessi sposi,* ("The Betrothed"). Although he always maintained that the two books should be regarded as complementing each other, they have been generally published as separate volumes. See Manzoni (1840).

30. Beccaria's position on equality before the law is also difficult and inconsistent. This passage seems to anticipate the position he took as a member of the com-

mission for the new Lombard Code, published in 1791. On that commission he contradicted the principle of equal law for all by advocating different punishments for different kinds of people: "the distinction of classes in the case of minor crimes is necessary in order to bring about the desired equality" (Maestro, 1973: 145)

31. That the classical school existed at all has been seriously challenged by Beirne (1993) largely because of his persuasive argument for the influence of the Scots on Beccaria, and it was the Scots more than any other contemporaries who stood for the application of science to the study of man and society.

32. Beccaria's views are probably close to "rule utilitarianism" which is not pure utilitarianism, but is primarily utilitarian nonetheless. Obedience to rules was an important and unstated assumption in many of the eighteenth-century utilitarian theorists. However, because of their adherence to the social contract they tended to see rules as an evil imposition, necessary only to maintain order, but certainly not as matters of morality in themselves (as argued by deontologists such as Kant).

33. This section, in part, draws on our article "Penological Reform and the Myth of Beccaria" (Newman and Marongiu, 1990)

34. It has been argued that Helvétius tried to practice in real life what he preached, so that his ideas were closely connected to the French revolution and also the English radicals such as John Wilkes (Wootton, 2000). In this sense Beccaria's *Treatise* is certainly indirectly relevant to practice, though in contrast to Helvétius (and of course Voltaire), Beccaria was much too timid to practice in the open his ideas. It should be added that Helvétius made a famous and humiliating retraction of his *Esprit* when it was first published, for fear of suffering the often severe reprisals from the Church.

35. In fact, Beccaria saw this problem, but insisted that, "… clemency is a virtue of the legislator and not of the administrator of the laws" in his Chapter XLVI on Pardons.

36. It should be noted that, with the exception of the pursuit of happiness, Bentham harshly criticized this passage, as he had also done concerning the French *Declaration of the Rights of Man*. Bentham was an outspoken critic of the American Declaration of Independence because it was based on the meaningless words of "life, liberty and property." Much later, after the successful American Revolution and the successful setting up of a democratic government, Bentham became instead a great admirer and supporter of the new American democracy. He wrote letters to Andrew Jackson, Thomas Jefferson and others urging them to adopt his criminal and legal codes, to which he received no response. To his chagrin, the American legal system continued to build on English common law, while at the same time developing its own legal codes.

37. To give just one example: "The New York loyalist Peter Van Schaack reached his decision to oppose Independence on the basis of a close and sympathetic reading of Locke, Vattel, Montesquieu, Grotius, Beccaria, and Pufendorf," (Bailyn, 1963:29)

38. See Mullett (1939-40) on the influence of the classics on the American revolutionary period and constitution.

39. The translation offered here is from the fourth edition by an unknown translator, currently introduced by Adolph Caso (1983). Our translation of the passage from Chapter XI on Disturbing the Peace is: "… if, by defending the rights of men and invincible truth, I have contributed to getting rid of the torments and distress of death that are put upon the unlucky victims of tyranny or ignorance—both equally fatal—I am so much consoled by the blessings and tears of just one innocent person moved to joy, even if I face the contempt of all mankind."

A Note on the Text

Endless speculations about the controversial genesis of the text of *On Crimes and Punishments* (hereinafter the *Treatise*) have surrounded its history, beginning with circumstances of Beccaria's life under which the project of the book took shape.

Having completed his formal education in his mid twenties, Beccaria became close friends with Pietro and Alessandro Verri, two brothers who formed, with a number of other young men from the Milan aristocracy, an intellectual circle *L'Accademia dei Pugni* (the Academy of Fists), interested in topics of socio-political and literary concern. Through this group Beccaria became acquainted with French and British political philosophers, such as Hobbes, Hume, Diderot, Helvétius, Montesquieu, and Hume. In March 1763, Pietro Verri asked Beccaria to prepare a critical report on the criminal justice system of the time. Although he had no experience in the administration of criminal justice, Beccaria accepted the assignment. Pietro's brother Alessandro, who had the official position of "protector of prisoners" in Milan assisted him with his knowledge and experience.

There is little doubt that the book was written with much encouragement and help from his friends in the Academy, especially from Pietro Verri who gave him the necessary background information, elaborated on the subject matter, substantially modified the original manuscript and eventually manually copied it, on request and with the explicit consent of Beccaria who, almost certainly, was not even present when the extensive corrections were made.

As we noted elsewhere (Newman and Marongiu; 1990, fn. 9), Nino Valeri, in his important biography of Pietro Verri writes: "[Verri] suggested to his friend, always weak and indecisive, the idea for the work... pushed him to write it, overcoming his natural laziness...Verri recopied in his own hand, the most confused pages.." (Valeri, 1969: 113, our translation). And further, "[Verri] was the loving obstetrician of a difficult birth..." (1969: 113, our translation). A letter written by Pietro Verri on November 1, 1765 describes the process in detail:

And now I will satisfy you on the subject of the book On Crimes and Punishments. The book is by the Marquis Beccaria. I gave him the subject; the majority of the ideas are the result of conversation which took place everyday between Beccaria, Alessandro, Lambertenghi and myself. In our society we pass the evening in the same room, each of us working. Alessandro is working on the Storia d'Italia, I have my political and economic works, Beccaria was bored and bored with others. Desperately, he asked me for a subject and I suggested this to him, because I knew it was an excellent one for an eloquent and very imaginative man. But he knew nothing about our criminal systems. Alessandro, who was Protector of Prisoners, promised to help him. Beccaria began to write his ideas on sheets of paper, and we encouraged him so much that he set down a great many ideas; every afternoon we took a walk and we talked of the errors in criminal law, we had discussions, questions, and then, at night, he did his writing; but it is so tiring for him to write that after an hour he cannot go on. When he had all the material collected, I wrote it down and we gave order to it, so to form a book. The difficulty was to publish such delicate matters without having trouble. I sent it to Mr. Aubert in Leghorn, who had published my *Meditazioni sulla felicità*. I sent the manuscript in April last year [1764] and we received the first copy in July 1764" (Maestro, 1942: 54).

A comparative analysis of the two original documents (Beccaria's autographed manuscript, consisting of a small leather volume, assembled by Beccaria's son Giulio, now in possession of the Biblioteca Ambrosiana, in Milan), actually shows that almost every section of the document was changed; entire passages of Beccaria's text were deleted or given a different meaning and many others added. The result was the beginning of the metamorphosis of the text, which would become complete with Morellet's version, of which we will discuss shortly.

The historical record also confirms that Verri's deep intervention in Beccaria's original project was made necessary by Beccaria's personality. Indeed the characterization of Beccaria as lazy, timid and reclusive is generally recognized. Cantù (1862: 153) describes Beccaria as solitary, shy and cowardly: "[Beccaria] … was careless in his handwriting and spelling... too lazy to write…" (*negletto nella scrittura e nell'ortografia... pigro nello scrivere..*). ."*.. had great difficulty in writing" (Cantù, 1862: 149). Romagnoli (1985: xxiv-xxvi) depicts Beccaria as "cowardly," "moody" (*pavido e ombroso*), "lazy and inept" (*pigrizia e inettitudine*), and "weak and indolent" (*debole e pigro*) (Our translations). Even Marcello Maestro (1942: 53) in his rather obsequious biography of Beccaria admits "… a tendency to laziness and melancholy, which was indeed a characteristic of [Beccaria's] temperament."

Some have argued that Pietro Verri exaggerated Beccaria's shortcomings out of envy for his growing international recognition and because Beccaria had not properly acknowledged his role in the creation of the book. Thus, Verri is a biased source. However, Beccaria's limited contribution to the production of the *Treatise* is generally acknowledged by his contemporaries. Marquis Freganeschi a very close friend of Pietro Verri, in another letter of January 18, 1783, for instance, made this caustic observation:*"Si ritiene il sig. Marchese Beccaria per autore del libro dei delitti e delle pene, quando sappiamo che quello che vi è di buono non è suo e quello che vi è di suo non è buono"* ("Signor Marchese Beccaria is regarded as the author of the book on crimes and punishments, while we do know that what is good in it, is not his, and what is his, is not good"—our translation). See: Francioni (1984: 217).

While the Verris always maintained that Beccaria's own manuscript was essentially not much more than a bunch of disorganized and virtually useless sheets or "scraps" of paper, Francioni (1984: 233-245) doggedly tried to demonstrate that this document, notwithstanding Beccaria's laziness and confusion in writing, showed an identifiable internal logic, which is quite different from the subsequent handwritten text of Verri. Francioni's basic assumption is that Beccaria's original intention was not to write a juridical treatise (acknowledging also his lack of specific background in the field), but rather a utilitarian styled pamphlet of moral and political philosophy about the role of the criminal justice system in fostering or impeding the progress of mankind towards "the greatest happiness for the greatest number." And being weak, Beccaria, could not resist Pietro Verri's tendency to turn the document into a more systematic juridical essay. This process can be understood in the context of the complex and very ambivalent relationship between Verris' dominant personalities and the passive Beccaria.

In any event, Beccaria eventually "produced" the first version of the book between March 1763 and January 1764. It is probable that most of the work was done in Pietro Verri's apartment in Milan after Beccaria's summer vacation, in about two months during the fall of 1763. The final manuscript was ready on February 29, 1764 and sent to Verri's publisher in Livorno, Giuseppe Aubert, on April 12, who, only a few months before had published Pietro Verris' *Meditazioni sulla felicità*. Verri's contribution to the production of the manuscript and the almost contemporaneous publication of the *Meditazioni*, have also spawned the speculation that they were both written by Pietro Verri.

The first edition of the book, reproducing with only minor modifications the Verris' manuscript, appeared in July of the same year in Livorno's printing office of Coltellini. The volume consisted of an Introduction, forty-one unnumbered chapters, 104 numbered pages, bore no bibliographical information, except the year and (in a few rare copies) an enclosed *errata corrige*. It was published anonymously, for security reasons, fearing some reprisal from catholic authorities. A few months after the first, a second "pirated" edition appeared in 1764 in Florence with the false bibliographical information of "In Monaco MDCCLXIV" and the notation *edizione seconda rivista e corretta*, and included a number of unauthorized corrections and printing errors. This was a counterfeited copy of the first edition, printed in Florence by Andrea Bonducci a few months later, probably in Fall 1764. A counterfeit of this counterfeited copy also appeared in the same year, possibly printed in Pisa or Livorno.

When a third edition of the *Treatise* was almost ready, in January 1765, as a result of the investigations of the Venetian Inquisition, Ferdinando Facchinei, a monk from Vallombroso produced a vehement pamphlet, accusing the author of sedition. This booklet, by the title, *Note ed osservazioni sul libro intitolato "Dei delitti e delle pene"* (Notes and Observations on the Book "On Crimes and Punishments), while arousing Beccaria's fear, provoked instead an immediate reaction of the Verri brothers. In only six days (January 15-21, 1765) they produced "Reply to a paper entitled : Notes and Observations on the Book 'On Crimes and Punishments'" (*Risposta ad uno scritto che s'intitola Note ed osservazioni sul libro "Dei delitti e delle pene"*), aimed to refute Facchinei's charges. This reply, entirely written by Pietro and Alessandro Verri, was immediately sent to the publisher, to be added in the forthcoming edition.

Eventually the third edition appeared,in Coltellini's printing office, Livorno in March 1765 (inscribed *IN LAUSANNA MDCCLXV*) with a number of additions of the author. Now four new chapters and twelve new passages were added, totaling 45 chapters. This includes the notation:

Terza Edizione rivista, corretta e notabilmente accresciuta dall'Autore, colle risposte dello stesso alle Note e Osservazioni Pubblicate in Venezia contro quell'Opera. Si aggiunge il Giudizio di un Celebre Professore (Third revised edition, with corrections and important additions by the author, including his reply to Notes and Observations Published in Venice against the Work. There is also the opinion of a Prominent Professor [Professor of Dialectics and Physics of Pisa University, Giovan Gualberto De Soria]).

This edition also shows the famous allegorical frontispiece, engraved by Giovanni Lapi, upon Beccaria's instructions, portraying Justice as rejecting the instruments of torture and capital punishment and looking with approval on the symbols of labor.

In 1765 Beccaria sent via d'Alembert a copy of the third edition to French Abbè André Morellet, who produced a French translation, which appeared in Paris on December 28, 1765 (with the false notation of *à Lausanne)*, introducing a number of substantial changes, altering its internal structure and the position of chapters and paragraphs, leaving only four paragraphs (III, IV, V, and XIX) in their original position. This version consists of 42 chapters showing a substantial redistribution of the text as follows (see: Francioni, 1984: 306-307):

- ten chapters are moved to a different position mostly without altering the content;
- five chapters are different from the Italian version because of internal transfer of sentences and new interpolations;
- ten chapters are supplemented with sentences taken from other chapters;
- nine chapters are "mutilated" by transposition of text to other chapters;
- two chapters are obtained by subtracting sentences from the original and replacing them with text from other chapters;
- six chapters are constructed by juxtaposition of different sentences from the same or from other chapters and one is created ex-novo, by isolating a portion of the text.

Such a substantial revision (and, according to many, "distortion") of the text can be easily understood as Morellet's attempt to produce a more rigorous juridical treatise than the one he had received and was translating. He perhaps took for granted that Beccaria had in mind such a project, because he was also working, as we have seen, on the available version of the book which had been already framed in juridical terms, due to Pietro Verri's initial intervention. It is therefore possible that Morellet simply decided to "improve" the *Treatise* according to this approach. The metamorphosis of *Dei delitti* was now complete.

Beccaria's attitude towards Morellet's version of the book was very ambivalent, resulting in significant contradictory behavior. On one hand he expressed appreciation to the French revision, by adding a note to the fifth edition of the *Treatise*, even asserting that "the French ordering is preferable to the author's own," while, on the other hand he did not include any of Morellet's changes in this very edition, which was published a few months later in March 1766 with a number of significant additions, including the important introductory note "To the Reader." Beccaria also, despite his manifestations of approval and of the presumed purpose of including Morellet's changes in the subsequent editions of the *Treatise*, constantly ignored the French ordering in all the Italian versions of the book that he personally edited, supervised and authorized. (A simple and perhaps obvious explanation could also be that he was too lazy to make the changes!) Whatever the reason, Beccaria's equivocal attitude towards the French version and subsequently his passive acceptance of the French-based Italian version of his book is at least partly responsible for the proliferation of subsequent versions in all languages, including Italian and English, derived from the reordered text.

Following his publisher Aubert's advice, from August 1765, Beccaria continued to work on the fifth edition of the book, even while another pirated edition (also called the fourth), virtually a mere reprinting of the third, appeared in mid 1765. The fifth edition was published in Livorno (Coltellini) March 1766, with the false place of publication of *Lausanna*. It included a number of significant additions, which included for the first time the name of Cesare Beccaria on the title page, the important introductory note "To the Reader" and two entirely new chapters: Revenue authorities and On Pardons (*Del fisco e Delle Grazie*), thus reaching forty-seven chapters. In this edition, Beccaria takes complete credit for the Verris' Reply to the Notes and Observations on the Book "On Crimes and Punishments" (*Risposta ad uno scritto che s'intitola Note ed osservazioni sul libro "Dei delitti e delle pene"*), which, as we saw above, was added to the third edition (March 1765). In the preface "To the Reader," he flatly states: "…. I have given public testimony of my religion and obedience to my sovereign in my reply to Notes and Observations..." As noted earlier, the Reply, aimed at refuting the charges of sacrilege and rebellion against authority raised against him by Ferdinando Facchinei, was entirely written by the Verri brothers.

Immediately after publication word came that the Sacred Congregation of the *Index Librorum Prohibitorum* had put the book on the Index. Because of this "incident," Beccaria and Aubert, made an attempt to withdraw all the copies from circulation, while at the same time hurriedly changing the front page. In this "new" version, which is in fact a manipulation of the same fifth edition, Beccaria's name disappeared and the *Lausanna* notation was changed into *Harlem*. Two counterfeit versions of the *Harlem* edition, (probably printed in Germany or Switzerland) appeared in the same period.

The "story" of the fifth *Harlem* edition, however was not finished. In the same year 1766, the publisher Giovan Claudio Molini produced one more virtually identical "French" version, called the sixth (*edizione sesta di nuovo corretta e accresciuta*), bearing the indication of *Harlem* and *A Paris*. A further counterfeited copy immediately followed. One more sixth edition was published in Italy in 1767, bearing the false place of origin of "Buglione." This is merely a reprinting of the fifth, but it includes Pietro Verri's *Meditazioni sulla Felicità* and a small essay on torture (*De tormentis*), written by Giovanni Venturini.

Two years later Aubert published his last edition of the *Treatise*, printed in 1769 by Coltellini in Livorno, bearing, as usual, the false indication of *Lausanna*. This *Edizione ultima dell'anno MDCCLXIX* includes an Italian translation of Voltaire's commentary to the *Dei delitti*, which had been written back in 1766, when the *Treatise* had become popular among French intellectuals, due to the Morellet translation. This commentary had been already included in some foreign editions of the *Treatise*, namely the French (*Philadelphiae, Yverdon:* 1766), the English (London, J. Almond: 1767), the Dutch (Amsterdam, G. Bon: 1768). Following this edition, at least six subsequent Italian versions would include Voltaire's commentary. The first edition in three volumes of the "complete works" of Beccaria appeared in Naples, in the printing office of Giovanni Gravier in 1770. This includes virtually everything Beccaria produced.

In 1774, bearing the false place of origin of *Londra* (London) there appeared an Italian version of the Morellet edition. This version was translated back into Italian, with some differences compared to the French text. It was printed in Livorno by Giovan Tomaso Masi who took over the former Coltellini firm. The several interpolations, relocations of portions of the text and even the presence of logical errors, according to Francioni (1984:320-21), made this edition much worse than all previous Italian and French editions. The name of the translator is unknown, though Firpo (1984: 513) suspects a Masi associate by the name of Gaetano Poggiali. This so-called *vulgata* represents an important step in the development of the *Treatise*, since from that moment on, all editions of Beccaria's text follow two distinct arrangements of the material: that edited by Beccaria himself, deriving from the 1766 fifth "Harlem" edition (in forty-seven chapters) and that of the *vulgata* (in forty-two chapters). According to Firpo (1984: 532-534), only in the eighteenth century, after the publication of the *vulgata*, out of a total of fourteen editions, eleven followed the French order. In the nineteenth and twentieth centuries at least fifty more "French" editions followed. Firpo (*ibidem*: 533) regrets that such "inauspicious" order had been accepted by many important editors of *Dei delitti,* such as Villari, Cantù, Mondolfo and Calamandrei. In other words the *vulgata* became the standard text for most subsequent Italian editions until 1958, when Franco Venturi produced the first modern Italian version of the *Treatise* using the fifth "Harlem" edition.

The first English translation of the *Treatise* was published in 1767 with the title: "An Essay on Crime and Punishment Translated from the Italian; with a Commentary attributed to Mons. De Voltaire Translated from the French (London: J. Almond)." This anonymous translation was followed the same year by another and then by several more editions in the subsequent decade. With minor differences this version comes from the original 1764 edition of the *Treatise*, with the addition of Voltaire's Commentary. It is interesting to note that, notwithstanding this addition, the unknown translator in his preface was very critical of Morellet's reordering, literally affirming that:

> He has assumed a right which belongs not to any translator, and which cannot be justified. His disposition may be more systematical, but certainly the author has as undoubted a right to the arrangement of his own ideas, as he has to the ideas themselves; and therefore to destroy that arrangement, is to pervert his meaning...

It should be noted that the English translator was certainly not alone in criticizing Morellet's ordering. In fact Diderot, along with other important personalities of the French Enlightenment, expressed the same opinion.

Firpo also notes (1984: 376, 375, fn. 6) that a complete appraisal of the numerous translations of the *Treatise* is still lacking. By 1984, twenty-two French, sixteen English, fourteen German, nine Spanish, six Russian, five Portuguese, three Hungarian, two Greek, two Polish, two Serbo-Croatian, two Swedish, one Danish, one Dutch, one Czech and one Turkish edition were recorded, but the list is far from complete. Eventually, the book appeared in twenty-two languages.

In conclusion, it seems virtually impossible to ascertain which of the several versions of the *Treatise* that appeared during his lifetime Beccaria considered as more closely reflecting his own thought and therefore should be regarded as "the real one." We have decided to base our translation on the Francioni (1984) text, by far the most exhaustive critical Italian edition of *Dei delitti e delle pene*. The Francioni text, like the one used by Venturi (1958, 1965) reproduces with negligible differences, the fifth,1766 "Harlem" version. The reason for this preference is essentially because this is undoubtedly the last edition that Beccaria personally oversaw and revised.

A final caution to the reader. In our notes to the translation, we constantly refer to "Beccaria" as though he had written every single word of the *Treatise*. Given the history of its creation, we know that this cannot be true. However, in the absence of further knowledge as to which parts he wrote and which parts the Verri brothers wrote, we have abided by the officially acknowledged authorship of Beccaria as a shorthand way of referring to the author or authors of the *Treatise*.

Biographical Note

Cesare Beccaria or Marchese Cesare Beccaria-Bonesana, the first son of an aristocratic, though not particularly wealthy, family, was born March 15, 1738 in Milan, where he grew up with two younger brothers (Francesco and Annibale) and a sister (Maddalena).

He started his formal education, at the age of eight, in the Collegio Farnesiano, a private Jesuit School in Parma. Later in his life he was very critical about the kind of education he received, describing it as "fanatical" and "servile." His talent both for foreign languages and mathematics was soon recognized, resulting in his nickname "Newtoncino"(little Newton). After some eight years in Parma, he entered Pavia University. Although not particularly distinguished as a student, he achieved his Law degree on September 13, 1758.

In 1761, he married Teresa Blasco against his parents' wishes and was constrained to live meagerly for a while without his family's support. His daughter Giulia, born in 1762, became the mother of Italian novelist and poet Alessandro Manzoni. She was the only child of this first marriage to survive Beccaria, since the others, Maria, Giovanni Annibale and Margherita all died very young.

During the winter 1761-62 (see: Note on the Text), Beccaria, with the brothers Pietro and Alessandro Verri, and other intellectuals formed a circle called "the academy of fists" which focused on topics of socio-political and literary interest. Through their literary magazine *Il Caffè*, modeled on Joseph Addison's English *Spectator*, they started an interesting and entirely new cultural reformist movement introducing in Italy important Enlightenment thinkers.

Beccaria wrote his first essay, in 1762, by the title of *Del disordine e de' rimedi delle monete nello stato di Milano nell'anno 1762.*("On Remedies for the Monetary Disorders of Milan in the Year 1762"), which was published in Lucca by Giuntini. His major work *Dei delitti e delle pene* was first published in Livorno in 1764 as noted previously in our Note on the Text. In 1764-65 Beccaria also published *Tentativo analitico su I contrabbandi* and another article for *Il Caffè*. (*I piaceri dell'immaginazione* and *Frammento sullo stile*).

The French Encyclopaedists invited Beccaria to France, following the success of *Dei delitti e delle pene,* Beccaria went to Paris but the visit was a complete failure. Due to his reclusive and timid personality, he hardly had any contact with the people who had invited him, and returned to Milan without finishing his trip. After the Paris trip he definitively broke with the Verri brothers, who in reprisal began to systematically denounce him. While there are different interpretations of this episode, it seems that one main reason for the Verris' resentment (especially Pietro) was the fact that Beccaria during and after the Paris trip did not acknowledge their considerable contribution to the *Treatise.* As noted earlier Beccaria also took complete credit for the extensive *Apologia*, entirely written by the Verri brothers in response to Facchinei's *Notes and Observations.*

Dei delitti e delle pene soon became famous and was publicly lauded by, among others, Katherine the Great who, in 1767, invited Beccaria to Russia as an official consultant on her project of penal reform. In character, Beccaria courteously declined this prestigious and tempting offer. And gradually, throughout France and England, an unfounded belief spread that Beccaria's failure to produce another work that could match *Dei delitti e delle pene* was due to the Austrian government's oppressive restrictions.

In November 1768 Beccaria was appointed to the chair of *scienze camerali* (law, public economy and commerce), founded expressly for him at the Palatine College of Milan, where he lectured for two years. His work in economic analysis is based primarily on these lectures, published after his death in 1804 under the title *Elementi di economia pubblica* (Elements of Public Economy). In 1770 he had published the first part of an essay by the title *Ricerche intorno alla natura dello stile* (Milano: Galeazzi). The second part was published posthumously in 1805. In 1771 he was appointed to the Supreme Economic Council of Milan and remained a public official for the rest of his life, filling a number of administrative assignments, ranging from monetary reform to trade, industry and agriculture. In 1791 he was appointed to the board for the reform of the judicial code and formulated a proposal for the abolition of capital punishment.

Beccaria's wife died on March 14, 1774. Eighty-two days later he married Anna dei Conti Barnaba Barbò and in 1775 a son, Giulio, was born. Beccaria's later years were troubled by family disputes and litigation on property and problems of health. He died in Milan on November 28, 1794, probably because of a stroke, following an attack of indigestion.

Cesare Beccaria

On Crimes and Punishments

Fifth edition with additions and corrections

Harlem 1766

In rebus quibuscumque difficilioribus non expectandum, ut quis simul, et serat, et metat, sed praeparatione opus est, ut per gradus maturescant.

In all negotiations of difficulty, a man may not look to sow and reap at once; but must prepare business, and so ripen it by degrees.
—Sir Francis Bacon[1] (Bacon, Serm. fidel., n. XIV)

To the Reader[1]

Begin with a few remnants of the laws of an ancient belligerent people compiled by a prince[2] who reigned Constantinople twelve centuries ago, add Lombardian customs,[3] and mix all these together into verbose and confused volumes by unknown authors. The tradition of opinions that results is what most of Europe still calls "law."[4] It is deplorably common even today that an opinion of Carpzov,[5] an ancient citation by Claro,[6] or a torture recommended with acrimonious complacency by Farinaccio[7] should make up the laws that are blindly followed by those people who ought only with great trepidation dispose of the lives and fortunes of men.[8] These laws, the dregs of the most barbarous of centuries, are examined in this book in respect to criminal justice.[9] We expose the defects of the criminal justice system to the officials responsible for social welfare, but we do it in a style that will not appeal to the ignorant or the impatient. The candid search for truth, and the independence from popular opinion that this work enjoys, are made possible by the kind and enlightened government under which the author lives. The great monarchs, the benefactors of humanity[10] who rule us, love the truths expounded even by obscure philosophers, but not with the fanaticism of those who favor force and fraud over reason. It will be clear to those who examine all the circumstances that the current confusion in criminal justice revealed in this book is the result of disparagement and criticism of previous ages, not of this century or its legislators.

Whoever should honor me with criticisms would do well to begin with a clear understanding of the goal of this work. It is a goal that, far from undermining legitimate authority, will serve to increase it—that is, if ideas are stronger than force, and if authority achieves recognition through mildness and humanity. The mistaken criticisms published against this book[11] are based upon confused notions, obliging me to interrupt for a moment my discourse with my enlightened readers, in order to erase once and for all the mistakes generated by the excessive zeal or calumny of malicious envy.

Moral principles and political order come from three sources: revelation, natural law,[12] and the accepted conventions of society. Of course, in regard to the primary role of revelation there is no comparison between it and the others, but they are similar in one respect: all three lead to happiness in this mortal life. To examine only the elements of the last of these three sources does not imply the exclusion of the other two. Revelation and natural law, although in principle divine and immutable, have been changed in a thousand ways by the false religions of men, and through the arbitrary notions of vice and virtue invented by their perverted minds. So it seems necessary to examine specifically human conventions that have been either explicitly formulated or assumed for reasons of common necessity and utility—an approach that every school of ethical thought and every system of morals must find agreeable.[13] It is always a worthy undertaking to compel even the most stubborn and skeptical to take note of the principles that induce men to live a social life. To continue, there are three separate classes of virtue and vice: religious, natural or dispositional and political.[14] These three classes should never be in contradiction with each other, but this does not imply that all the consequences and duties following from the one necessarily derive from the others. Natural law does not explain everything that is explained by revelation, nor does pure social law explain all of natural law.[15] However, it is very important to study separately the products of human conventions, (that is the expressed or tacit agreements among men) because they provide the limits to what one man can lawfully do to another without a special sanction from the supreme being. Thus, the idea of political virtue may be clearly deemed to vary; the idea of natural virtue[16] would be clear and apparent if not for the stupidity and emotionality of men; and the idea of religious virtue is always there, directly revealed and preserved by God.[17]

Therefore it would be wrong to accuse one who speaks of social conventions and their consequences, of being opposed to natural law or to revelation, for he does not speak of these. It would be wrong, when speaking of the state of war that existed before society came into being, to assume that it was the Hobbesian state of nature bereft of any overriding human duty or obligation.[18] Rather, the state of nature that preceded society was born by the corruption of human nature and lack of a clear direction from above. Finally, it would also be wrong to criticize an author who studies the effects of the social contract for failing to recognize that these "effects" could have existed before the social contract itself.[19]

Because divine justice and natural justice are in essence unchangeable and constant, the relationship between them always remains the same.

But human justice—or more accurately political justice—represents the fleeting relationships between the actions of men and a constantly changing society. Thus human justice will change depending on whether the action in question is essential or useful to society. But these links between action and society are not readily discernible without careful analysis of the infinitely complex arrangements of civil society. Once these principles of human justice are confused with divine and natural justice there is no hope for reason in public affairs. It is up to theologians to establish the boundaries of injustice and justice in respect to the intrinsic evil or goodness of an act. It is up to the experts[20] of public law and the State to denote the domains of political justice and injustice—that is what is useful or harmful to society. Nor can the project of one type of justice interfere with the other, since everyone understands how much purely political virtue must surrender to the immutable virtue that emanates from God.[21]

To repeat: whoever would honor me with criticisms, don't start by accusing me of principles destructive of virtue or religion, for I have shown that I hold no such position. Furthermore, instead of making me out as an unbeliever and seditious person, identify my poor logic or careless analysis of public affairs; and do not tremble at my every proposition that actually supports the needs of humanity. Rather, convince me of the uselessness of my principles or of the political damage that will arise from them; convince me of the superiority of established practices. I have given public testimony of my religion and obedience to my sovereign in my reply to *Notes and Observations*.[22] To answer further queries similar to those would be superfluous. But whoever will write with the decency that is worthy of honest men and with the intelligence that recognizes the futility of making me prove over and over my basic premises[23]— no matter who they are—will find in me not so much a man who searches for a slick answer, but a peaceful man devoted to the truth.[24*]

---

*   *Author's note:* Everything contained with this sign [ ] was added in the first revision made to the text. Anything contained within this sign [[ ]] was added for the second revision.

**   These are Beccaria's additions to the second and third edition of the *Treatise* both published in Livorno in 1764 and 1765, respectively bearing the false place of impression of Monaco and Lausanna (see: Note to the Text).

Introduction

Men typically leave the most important regulation of their lives to the everyday direction and discretion of those whose interests are opposed to the most beneficial laws. These laws should serve universal interests and resist the pressure for power to become concentrated among the few who reap its benefits, leaving the rest of the people weak and miserable.[1] Thus do ordinary men, only after having lived through many deceptions concerning the most basic matters of life and liberty, weary of the evils they have suffered, finally reaching the limits of endurance, come to redress the disorders that oppress them. They begin to recognize the most obvious of truths, the very simplicity of which escapes understanding by the crude minds that are not accustomed to objective analysis and that receive without question the prepackaged impressions of tradition.

History tells us that laws are, or ought to be, the result of agreements among free men, but that they have mostly served the interests of an ardent few.[2] Or, they have been formed from the accidental necessities of daily life. Certainly, laws have never been constructed according to the scientific study[3] of human nature, which would comprehend in totality the actions of the multitude of individuals in society. If it were so, one clear proposition would follow: *the greatest happiness*[4] *for the greatest number*.[5] How fortunate are those few nations that did not wait for the slow changes that depend on accidents or human foibles, and succeeded in transforming the excesses of evil into good, even hastening the passage through the intermediate stage of development to good laws.[6] Indeed, we all owe a debt of gratitude to the philosopher[7] who courageously labored in obscurity and isolation in his small study, to spread the first seeds of useful truths that had remained dormant for so long.

We are now able to identify the specific links between sovereign and subject, and among nations. Commerce has flourished thanks to the dissemination of philosophical truths via the news media,[8] and a quiet commercial rivalry among nations has arisen, a healthy competition[9] worthy of rational men. These are the fruit of our enlightened century. Yet given these accomplishments, few have scrutinized or questioned the cruelty of punishment and the irregularities of criminal procedure—the part of legislation that is so important and so neglected nearly everywhere in Europe. Very few have thought to return to basic principles in order to eradicate the accumulated errors[10] of many centuries, or at least to use the persuasiveness that only acknowledged truth can provide to curb the rampant course of misguided power—power that has achieved the "legitimacy" of detached atrocity. Surely the cries of the weak, sacrificed to plain ignorance and smug indifference; surely the barbaric tortures lavishly and uselessly multiplied for crimes never proven or crimes even imagined; surely the squalor and horror of prison made worse by uncertainty that is the cruelest tormentor of the wretched, surely all these instances are enough to shake up those magistrates who lead the opinions of men.

The immortal President Montesquieu[11] has touched lightly on this subject. Truth alone has forced me to follow the shining footsteps of this great man. However, the thinking men for whom I write will easily distinguish my approach from his.[12] I will be very fortunate indeed if I can earn, as did he, the personal gratitude of the modest and peaceful devotees of reason, and if I am able to inspire that sweet thrill experienced by sensitive minds when they respond to one who cares for the interests of all humanity!

§ I. The Origin of Punishments

Laws are the means by which independent and isolated individuals, tired of living in a continuous state of war and of enjoying a liberty made useless by the uncertainty of having constantly to defend it, are united into a society. Individuals sacrifice a part of their liberty in order to enjoy the rest of it in peace and safety. The sum of all these individual portions of liberty sacrificed for the good of all constitutes the sovereignty of a nation, of which the sovereign is the legitimate owner and administrator.[1] But it is not enough just to create a depositary of the common good, because it has to be defended against individual usurpations, and because all individuals would, if they could, not only try to retrieve their own portion of the depositary, but would also appropriate that of others. Thus, concrete incentives are necessary to dissuade the despotic mentality of every individual from thrusting the laws of society back into a prehistoric chaos. These incentives become the punishments carried out against those who break the law. I say these are *"concrete incentives"*[2] because experience tells us that the masses do not, of their own, display stable principles of conduct. Thus, the universal principle of dissolution observed in both the physical and moral worlds can only be avoided, in the case of society, by the use of punishments that directly strike the senses and lodge themselves in the mind to neutralize the individual passions that are the enemy of the common good. Not big speeches, strong words, or even the most sublime truths are enough over any considerable length of time to quell the passions excited by the demand for immediate gratification.[3]

§ II. The Right to Punish

Every punishment that does not derive from absolute necessity, says the great Montesquieu,[1] is tyrannical. This proposition may be stated as a general principle: every act of coercion of one man against another that does not derive from absolute necessity is tyrannical. Such is the foundation of the sovereign's right to punish crimes: the necessity to defend the depositary of public welfare against the usurpation by individuals. In addition, the more just are the punishments, the more sacred and inviolable is the public trust, and the greater the liberty that the sovereign preserves for his subjects. When we consult the human heart, we find the fundamental principles of the genuine right of the sovereign to punish crimes, because one cannot expect a lasting advantage of political morality if such morality is not founded on the immutable sentiments of man. Laws that deviate from these sentiments will always meet with resistance that will eventually overthrow them—in the same way as a force, however slight, when continually applied will overcome a violent motion applied to a physical body.

No man has ever freely given up a part of his personal liberty for the public good. Such a chimera exists only in novels. If it were possible, every one of us would wish that the agreements that bind other men did not bind ourselves. Every man acts as though he were the center of the world's affairs.

[The increase in human population, though slight, nevertheless was too much for the scarcity and harshness of nature to satisfy the needs of all. These individual needs inevitably become interrelated and for this reason the first savages banded together. As these first collectives formed, other groups formed to resist them, and so the state of war was transported from individuals to nations.][2]

It was necessity, then, that forced men to give up part of their personal liberty. Hence, it is certain that each man wanted to put into the public depositary the smallest portion of his liberty possible, only enough to induce others to defend it. The aggregate of these smallest possible portions constitutes the right to punish.[3] Everything beyond that is abuse

11

and not justice. It may even be a fact, but that does not make it a right. Note that the word *right* does not contradict the word *force*, rather the former is a modification of the latter—in other words it is a modification that truly serves the greater number. And by "*justice*" I mean no more than the constraint that is necessary to hold individual interests together, without which they would fall back into a primitive antisocial state. All punishments that go beyond what is necessary to conserve this bond are inherently unjust. One must be careful not to attach to this word "justice" the idea that it is something real, like a physical force or something that actually exists. It is simply a way of thinking, a way that infinitely affects the happiness of everyone. Of course, I do not here speak of the kind of justice that emanates from God and that is directly linked to the punishments and rewards of the after-life.

§ III. Implications So Far

The most important implication that follows from these principles is that only the law may decree the punishment of crimes,[1] and this authority resides with the legislator who represents society as a whole in accordance with the social contract. Thus no judge, who is part of society after all, may justly inflict punishment on another member of that same society unless it is within the limits prescribed by law.[2] Certainly, a judge is never justified in inflicting a punishment against a delinquent citizen beyond that fixed by law, even if done with excessive zeal under the pretext of the public good.

The second implication is that each and every individual is bound to society which in turn is bound to each of its members, a bond which nature dictates. It represents an obligation* that reaches from the throne to the hovel, applying equally to the most privileged and the most miserable of men. Indeed it would be a trivial obligation if it were not for the fact that it serves the interests of all by acknowledging the consensus of the majority.[3] The violation of this rule alone would start down the path to anarchy. Furthermore, the sovereign, who represents that same society may make only general laws that bind all individuals to society. However, he must never make a judgment against an individual who violated the social contract, because then the nation would be divided into two parts, one supporting the sovereign, the other supporting the accused. It is therefore necessary that a third party adjudge the facts. Hence the necessity for a judge whose decisions cannot be appealed, and that consist only of affirmations or negations of particular facts.[4.]

Author's note: [The word obligation is one of those terms much more frequently used in ethics than in any other science and is here essentially an abbreviation for a process of reasoning rather than designation of an idea. If you look for an idea corresponding to the word obligation, you will not find it; but if you reason about it you will understand and be understood.]

Translators' note: In this rather obscure passage, Beccaria tries to define "obligation" not as a metaphysical concept but as a rational convention according to the principle of utility, i.e., it is not an arbitrary moral principle, but a choice that individuals make that is, on balance, for their own good and that of others. See the Introduction to the Treatise, especially in regard to its significance for Bentham. In the following chapter Beccaria examines more closely the origins of "obligation."

The third implication is that, even if a terrible punishment is not clearly opposed to the public good since it aims ultimately to deter crimes, it still remains contrary to the moral values of enlightened reason. Rather than crudely commanding a sullen mob of slaves, perpetuating a cycle of cruelty in the name of justice, an enlightened ruler looks on happy men in a just society that reflects the social contract.

§ IV. The Interpretation of Laws

The fourth implication. Judges do not have the authority to interpret the laws for the simple reason that they are not legislators. Nor have judges received the laws from our dead ancestors according to domestic tradition as though left to them in a will which they must obey. Rather, they receive laws from a living society or its sovereign, as the genuine representatives of the will of all, not in strict obligation[1] to a vow, which the ancients were incapable of agreeing to anyway. Incapable because the ancient vow presumed to bind wills that did not then exist thus imposing slavish obedience that reduced a society of men to that of a herd. However, it is the lingering effects of this profound feeling of obedience that motivates living subjects to freely unite in solidarity with the sovereign, understanding that this is necessary to keep the internal ferment and selfishness of human nature under control. This is the truly physical root of legal authority. Who, then, should be the legitimate interpreter of laws? The sovereign who is the depositary of the actual will of all citizens, or the judge, who alone examines whether another man has or has not broken the law?

A judge must approach every criminal case using an exact syllogism that moves from the general to the particular: (1) The major premise asks what the law says about this case; (2) the minor premise asks how the facts match the law; (3) the conclusion is the decision of either liberty or punishment. When a judge deviates from this syllogism, claiming that the facts demand it, he opens the door to uncertainty.[2]

Nothing is more dangerous than the common belief that a judge must abide by the "spirit of the law." Doing so opens the floodgate to a torrent of opinions. This truth seems paradoxical to laymen, who are more concerned with trivial disorders of the moment, rather than the fatal long term consequences born of a false belief. Our consciousness and all of our ideas are highly interconnected and very complicated by the numerous paths by which men reach their conclusions. Each person has his own point of view; and even this may change at different times. The spirit of the law, therefore, results from the good or bad logic of the judge;

which may in turn depend on his good or bad digestion, or the intensity of his emotions, or the demeanor of the accused and his connection to the judge; and on all of those small appurtenances that change the appearance of objects in the constantly fluctuating minds of men. Thus, the fate of citizens is determined after many visits to different courts, their miserable lives victimized by the false logic of judicial procedures and even the heated sentiments of the judge. They are fooled into taking as legitimate the vague outcome of this confused series of notions and mental machinations. Thus, the courts issue different punishments for the same crimes and at different times, without consulting what the law actually prescribes, as they lurch into inconsistent interpretations of the law.

The disorder caused by the rigorous adherence to the letter of the law is insignificant compared to that caused by its interpretation. The former is a temporary inconvenience that can be corrected easily by making the necessary changes to the law. But the latter is the cause of uncertainty that severely impedes reason resulting in arbitrary and venal arguments. When there is a fixed legal code, it must be observed to the letter, and the judge must not be permitted to do anything else except examine the actions of the accused and decide whether or not they violate the law as it is written. Only then will the rule of law apply equally to ignorant citizens or the city fathers. When a just decision is not a matter of controversy but of facts, the accused will not be subjected to the fickle tyrannies of the many which can be worse than the cruelty of a single despot, particularly as a single despot is more easily held accountable than is the despotism over many which is less visible because despots are, in fact, closer in status to those whom they ravage.[3] Furthermore, the cruelty of a despot is conditioned by the obstacles he faces, not by the power that he wields. In this way citizens receive security for themselves that is right because it is in keeping with their standing in society, and is useful because it precisely accounts for the inconveniences caused by a misdeed. It is also true that citizens acquire a spirit of independence, not driven by resentment against the laws or recalcitrance against the chief judges, but by a healthy wish to denounce, in the sacred name of virtue, the weaknesses that result from selfishness or capricious opinion. Those who administer the law by assigning to the accused the wounds of tyranny will regret these principles. Indeed, I should become most afraid if the "spirit of tyranny" were to become one and the same with the spirit of an informed citizenry.

§ V. The Obscurity of the Laws

If the interpretation of the laws is bad, it is even more evident that their obscurity inevitably makes it so, and is made worse when the laws are written in a language that is foreign to ordinary people. This makes them dependent on the few insiders, unable to judge for themselves the threats to their own or others' liberty, overwhelmed as they are by the solemnity of bookish language. What should we think of these insiders who stand for the most cultured and illuminated of all Europe? Let there be no doubt that ignorance and uncertainty about punishment will incite the eloquence of passions. So the greater the number of those who ponder and hold in their frail hands the sacred code of laws, the fewer crimes there will be.

One consequence of this last reflection is that without written laws a society can never have an enduring form of government in which power is wielded by everyone, in contrast to laws that serve a minority, laws that are unalterable by the general will, or are contaminated by the foibles of private interests. Experience and reason show us that the future and certainty of humane practices are diminished according to how far they are from their source.[1] For if there is no solid foundation to the social contract how will laws resist the pressures brought on by the inevitable force of time and of passions?[2]

From this we can see how important is the printing press that makes the public the true repository of laws, rather than letting it be confined to just a few. And we can see how this public spirit can cut through the murk of cabals and intrigue, by confronting them with the enlightenment and with science which they scorn but really fear. This is the reason why we have seen in Europe a reduction in the atrocity of crimes suffered by our forefathers who have been through both tyranny and slavery. Anyone acquainted with the history of the last two or three centuries, including our own, can see how the sweetest virtues of humanity, kindness and tolerance of human error, were born in the midst of luxury and soft heartedness. But he will also see the effects of what is wrongly called good old fashioned simplicity and faith: humanity struggles under the

17

weight of superstition; greed and selfish ambition pursue chests of gold and the thrones of kings stained with blood; secret betrayals and public butchery; every noble a tyrant, ministers of the Gospel touching the God of meekness every day with bloody hands. Surely these are not the product of this enlightened century that some call corrupt!

§ VI. The Proportion between Crime and Punishment

Not only is it in the common interest that crimes are not committed, but when they are, the evil brought on society should be the least possible. Thus, the obstacles that deter men from committing crimes must correspond both to the amount of harm done to society, and the degree of temptation[1] faced by the offender. Therefore, there must be a fixed proportion between crime and punishment.[2]

It is impossible to prevent all disorder that results from the universal tussle of human passions. Disorder increases in correspondence to population increase and the complex give and take of private interests. This correlation between disorder and the state of society must be assessed in terms of a political probability because the exact mathematical relationship cannot be determined. [[A cursory look at history reveals that disorder increases as empires expand their boundaries during periods of particular rulers, and the corresponding national sentiment decreases accordingly, which causes crimes to increase. Because of this increase in crime, everyone takes more interest in crime and disorder so there is always a pressure to increase punishment.]][3]

This force is like gravity which pushes us for our own good, but if unrestrained, obstacles must be placed in our way. The effects of this force are a confused series of actions: if these clash directly into each other and crimes result, punishment, or what I call *political obstacles*[4] are necessary to impede the evil result without destroying the original force which is, after all, part and parcel of human nature. The legislators must become skilled architects whose duty it is to oppose the ruinous direction of gravity and to plot against those contributing to its consolidation.

Given the necessity to unite individuals in society, given agreements among men that necessarily lead to conflict between private interests, there must be established a scale of disorders ranging from the most serious that immediately destroy society,[5] to the least serious that do minimal harm or injustice to private individuals. Between these two extremes are all the acts that oppose the public good, which we call crimes, and these should be graded objectively from the highest to the lowest in severity. If geometry could be adapted to the infinite and hardly observable complexities of human action, it would be possible to construct a scale of corresponding punishments, descending from the strongest to the weakest, but it would be sufficient for a wise legislator to identify the principle points of correspondence, without upsetting the ordering of seriousness of crimes and punishments from the highest to the lowest If we could do an exact scale of the universe of punishments and crimes we would probably end up with a single scale of tyranny to liberty, and ultimately of the range of humanity and evil of different nations.

Any action that does not fall between the two extremes is not a *crime* nor can it be punished as such, except by those who have a personal interest in making it so. The doubt about these limits has produced in nations a moral climate that opposes legislation implementing them, and much legislation that excludes the reciprocity between crime and punishment. Others have produced a multitude of laws that end up exposing the wisest men to the most severe punishments. In fact, their doubts cause them to waffle even about what the words *vice* and *virtue* stand for, or even whether they exist. The result is chronic inaction and a fatal somnolence in the body politic. Whoever reads the legal codes and records of nations from a philosophical viewpoint will always find that the words *vice* and *virtue* of a *good* or *bad* citizen change with the revolutions of the period, not because of the changes in circumstances that occur in countries (which would be for the common interest), but because of the passions and human errors that successively agitated different legislators. He would easily see that the passions of one period formed the basis of morality of future periods, and that violent passions, the daughters of fanaticism and enthusiasm, enfeebled by time, reduce all physical and moral phenomena to one and the same, producing little by little the wisdom of the period, but also providing a very useful instrument in the hand of a strong and shrewd individual. In this way the most obscure notions of honor and virtue were born, and will remain so because their meanings change with the revolutions of time so that the words no longer carry their original meaning. They change as do rivers, hills and the boundaries of states which represent not only a physical but a moral geography.[6]

If pleasure and pain are the engine of our sensibilities,[7] and rewards and punishments are among the motives designated by the hidden legislator to compel men to accomplish the most sublime works, the inexact distribution of these rewards and punishments will result in the common but little recognized contradiction, that of punishment punishing the crimes it has caused.

But if the same punishment is given for two different crimes men will not be deterred from committing the more serious of the two crimes and will gain advantage by doing so.[8]

§ VII. Errors in the Measurement of Crime[1]

The preceding considerations allow me to assert that a unique and true measure of crimes is the harm done to society,[2] and that those who assign the true measure of crimes to the intent of the offender are mistaken. The latter depends entirely on the assessment of the motive that derives from a psychological predisposition and this is different for each and every man, because of the swift succession of ideas, passions and circumstances. Thus, it would be necessary to construct a legal code for each different citizen for every new law for every crime. Sometimes men with good intentions perpetrate the worst evils on society and at other times the more evil often do greater good.

Others measure crimes according to the dignity of the victimized person—who measures the damage to the public good according to his own importance. If this were the true measure of crimes, then the slightest irreverence to the divine Being should be punished infinitely more than the assassination of a monarch.

Finally, others think that the gravity of sin should inform the measurement of the seriousness of crimes. The fallacy of this opinion is readily apparent to the detached observer of the true relationships between man and man and between man and God. First, relationships of equality. The clash of passions and opposing interests is the sole reason for the idea of *common utility*, which is the basis of all human justice. The second are the relationships of dependence with the perfect Being and creator, who has reserved for himself the right to be legislator and judge of all time, because he is the only one who can do it without difficulty. He decrees divine punishment for an eternity to those who disobey him. What insect or supplicant to divine justice would question his omnipotence, when it is he alone who can act without being acted upon, and who has no sensation of pleasure or pain? The gravity of sin thus depends on the unfathomable evil of the human heart. This cannot be known without divine revelation. How then can we derive norms for the punishment of crimes? Should men be able to punish when God forgives and forgive when God punishes? If men may contradict the Omnipotent in offending him, they are able also to punish him.

23

§ VIII. The Classification of Crimes

We have seen that the true measure of crime is *the harm done to society*. This is one of those palpable truths which does not need quadrants or telescopes to discover it, and, understandable by any ordinary person, is known by a curious combination of circumstances only to a very few thinking men in every nation and every century. The contrary opinions, reminiscent of Asia,[1] are passions dressed up as authority with the power to drive man's sensibilities most of the time, making violent impressions on their weak will, overrunning the simple notions that perhaps formed the first philosophy of an emerging society. The current century seems to hark back to those simple notions but is more resolute because it is able to apply more incisive thinking, conditioned by thousands of baleful experiences and obstacles that had to be overcome. A systematic approach would now oblige us to examine and identify all the different sorts of crimes and how they should be punished. However, nature is so variable and circumstances change so much according to time and place that to do this would result in a work of immensely boring detail.[2] I think it is enough to outline the general principles and uncover the more common errors which would undermine the love of liberty and lead to anarchy, thus pleasing those who would reduce men to be regulated like the columns in a cloister.

Some crimes directly destroy society or its representative; some upset the secure lives of private citizens for gain or for honor; other actions may or may not oblige us to make laws from the point of view of the common good.[3] First, the most serious crimes, because they do the most damage, are called *Lèse Majesté*.[4] In giving it this name tyranny and ignorance confuse the terms and meaning of this crime which demands the maximum of punishment. Thus, many men are victimized by a word and receive the maximum punishment regardless of the thousand different circumstances in which the crime occurs.[5] Every crime that is kept private may be seen to offend society, but not every such crime threatens immediate destruction of society. Moral actions, as in physics, are self regulating and are circumscribed in many diverse ways in time and space, as are all movements in nature. Thus only a sophistic interpretation that is worthy of the philosophy of slaves manages to confound eternal truth with the distinct and enduring relationships[6] discovered over time.

After these follow the crimes that threaten the security of each individual. Since security is the primary reason for all legitimate associations one must assign some of the more severe punishments established by law to violations that threaten every citizen's right to security.

The opinion that everyone must have the power to do anything that is not against the law without fear of inconveniences except those caused by the act itself, should be a popular political tenet shared by honest magistrates who should promote it with the incorruptible administration of the law throughout society. It is a sacred tenet without which there would be no legitimate society, a just reward for the sacrifice of liberty made by all men in universal affirmation of the common needs of every sentient being, these actions limited only by individual ability. It is a process that opens minds to vigorous and clear thinking, making men virtuous in the process. This virtue also knows how to resist fear, unlike malleable prudence that is destined to suffer in a precarious state of uncertainty. Therefore, the assault against the security and liberty of citizens is one of the more serious crimes. Within this class fall not only assassinations and robberies by ordinary men, but also those crimes by persons of high position and judges, whose actions set a forceful and terrible example, destroying in their subjects the idea of justice and putting in its place rule by force, dangerous both to those who exercise it and those who suffer it.

§ IX. Honor

There is a remarkable contradiction between civil laws, the zealous guardians of the life and limb of all citizens, and the laws that defend what is called *honor* which is governed by personal belief. This word *honor* is the subject of long and brilliant debates, but it is incoherent and has no link to any established idea. How miserable is the condition of the human mind that goes to such lengths in comprehending the least important ideas, such as the revolution of the celestial bodies, in preference to understanding problems close to home; problems so pertinent to the most important notions of morality. Minds constantly vacillating and confused according to how the winds of passion blow, received and regurgitated by their ignorance! But this apparent paradox disappears if one considers that, just as objects that are too close to the eyes become blurred, so the simplest ideas that form the basis of morality are confused together because they are too close for comfort, with the result that the precision necessary to delineate the phenomena of human sensibilities is lost. And the detached student of all things human will no longer be amazed to find that there is no need for such a monstrous apparatus of so many restraints to keep men happy and secure.

Honor, then, is one of those complex ideas that are composed not only of simple ideas, but also of a complex process in which one idea is accepted at one time, at another time it is rejected, and at other times diverse ideas are mixed together. But none of the simple ideas that are for the common good are conserved, so great is the algebraic complexity of this mixture for want of a common divisor. But to find this common divisor in the diversity of many ideas that men have of honor, one must briefly look back to the original formation of society. The first laws and the first judges were born of necessity to give shelter against the disorder caused by the intrinsic physical despotism of every man.[1] This was a small step towards the creation of society, always thought of, whether real or imagined, as the testament to all legal codes even those that were destructive. Later as men had more to do with each other they grew more intelligent, thus creating an infinite series of social actions expressing their reciprocal needs, often taking the place of laws which were actually inferior to the power of these informal relationships among men. In this first period, primitive beliefs[2] dominated men's thinking, and were the single means of obtaining from others their good will, and keeping evil at bay, which the laws were not able to do. These elementary beliefs that tormented both the wise and the vulgar, replaced virtue itself with the appearance of virtue, which actually represented wickedness because it did not serve the true interests of the people. Thus, the "rights"[3] of individuals served a useful even necessary purpose by saving them from sinking below a commonly accepted level of behavior. Thus, ambition and conquest functioned to transform vanity into merit, with the honor of every man seen as unassailable. This *honor* it has become the entire *raison d'être* of many men's lives. Born after the formation of society it is not able to serve the common good, in fact is really a return to the state of nature and a temporary setback from the development of laws that are able to sufficiently defend the ordinary citizen.

Hence the ideas of honor are buried in an extreme political liberty and extreme state of dependence, totally mixed up with other ideas; because first, the despotism of laws made it useless to look to them to defend the rights of others, and second the despotism of men erased any idea of civil life among them, reducing them to people of shallow and fleeting character. Honor is, then, one of the fundamental principles of monarchies, which are forms of mitigated despotism, and it has in it the same role that revolutions have in despotic states,[4] that is a momentary return to the state of nature, a reminder to the ruler of the ancient equality of men.[5]

§ X. Duels

From this demand for respect from others, private duels were born, which owe their origin to the anarchy of laws. It is claimed that duels were unknown in antiquity, perhaps because our forefathers, always suspicious, did not go armed in their temples or theaters or among friends; or perhaps because free men would not deign to admit that the duel was a frequent and common spectacle of debased slave gladiators, and free men disdained to be considered and called gladiators because of their private combat. Laws decreeing death for he who accepts a duel have tried in vain to eradicate this custom, but it is so much a part of a man's identity that he fears loss of respect before others more than death. The man of honor is exposed to his fate all alone, a terrible state for a social being, and becomes the target of insults and infamy, repeated over and over which entirely overshadows any fear of punishment. So why do common people generally duel less than those of higher status? It is not only because commoners are not armed, but also because the need for the respect of others is less among commoners than for the upper class who look on each other with more suspicion and jealousy.

There is no need to repeat at this point what others have written, which is that a better method to prevent this crime is to punish the aggressor, the one who has demanded the duel, and to declare innocent he who is without blame when he is forced to defend something that existing laws do not guarantee—his reputation—and he has to show that he fears only the law, not men.

§ XI. Disturbing the Peace

Finally, crimes of the third kind[1] are those that disturb the peace and quiet of citizens. These include the clamor and merrymaking that disturbs commerce and the peaceful passage of citizens and the fanatical sermons that easily incite the passions of a curious multitude, sermons that force their mystical excitement and obscurity on deaf ears, rather than by calm and clear reason which cannot penetrate the masses.

Useful means to prevent the danger of intensifying public passions include: the illumination of public places at night; placement of guards in different quarters of the city; simple moral discourses on religion offered in silence and the tranquility of churches at public expense; and lectures designed to sustain different interests at public meetings of nations and parliaments or the sovereign's court. These preventive measures should form the main part of the duties of a magistrate, whom the French call *police*, but if this magistrate acts arbitrarily and inconsistently interprets the legal code which should reflect the wishes of all citizens, he opens a door to tyranny, which always encapsulates political liberty. I see no exception to this general axiom, that all citizens must know when they are guilty and when they are innocent.[2] If censors, and in general judicial arbitrators, are necessary in every government, this necessity was born from the frailty of its constitution and not from the nature of a well organized government. Deep uncertainty of one's own fate has sacrificed more victims to the darkness of tyranny than even public and solemn cruelty. It stirs these awakenings more than debasing them. True tyranny always begins with the domination of primitive beliefs, challenging courage which cannot shine except in the clear light of truth, when faced with the fire of passions and ignorance of danger.

But what should be the punishments for these crimes? Is death a punishment *truly useful and necessary* for the security and good order of society? Are torture and torment truly *just*, and do they fulfill the *goal* proclaimed by the laws? What is the better way to prevent crimes? Are these same punishments equally applicable to every time and circumstance? How much influence should customs have? These problems should be considered with a geometric precision to which sophism, seductive eloquence and timid doubt will succumb. I consider myself fortunate, if for no other reason that I am the first in Italy to present with much evidence what other nations have written or practiced. But if, by defending the rights of men[3] and invincible truth, I have contributed to getting rid of the torments and distress of death that are put upon the unlucky victims of tyranny or ignorance—both equally fatal—I am so much consoled by the blessings and tears of just one innocent person moved to joy, even if I face the contempt of all mankind.

§ XII. The Purpose of Punishment

From these simple considerations of truth now set forth it is obvious that the purpose of punishment is not to inflict torment and pain on a sentient being, nor to undo the crime that has already been committed. Is it possible in a body politic, having for a long time acted passionately, to act as a calm moderator of these passions, to harness this cruel instrument of fury, the fanaticism of impotent tyrants? Can it erase the past squeals of unhappiness when it is not possible to take back the actions already consummated? The purpose, then, is none other than to prevent the action from doing further damage to our citizens and to prevent others from doing the same thing. Thus, punishments, and the method of inflicting them must be chosen according to the amount needed to make an impression more useful and more lasting on the minds of men, and less to torment the body of the offender.[1]

§ XIII. On Witnesses

There is a set procedure in all quality legislation for determining precisely the credibility of witnesses and for verifying the facts of the crime. Any reasonable man, whose ideas are logically expressed and whose sensibilities are similar to those of other men, may be a witness. [[The true measure of his credibility is nothing other than his interest in telling or not telling the truth. Thus, it is frivolous to reject women who are seen as weak witnesses, puerile to equate the effects of real death to those of civil death,[1] and ridiculous to reject the infamous because of their infamy when they have no interest in lying.]] The credibility of witnesses, then, should diminish in proportion to their hatred, friendship, or other direct relationships to the accused. More than one witness is necessary, because the assertion of one person does not prove anything, especially as the rule of law demands that one is innocent until proved guilty. The credibility of a witness decreases in proportion to the horror of the crime[*] or the improbability of the circumstances, such as for example, witchcraft or gratuitously cruel actions. In the case of witchcraft it is more likely that

---

[*] *Author's note*: [[According to criminal lawyers, the credibility of a witness varies in proportion to the seriousness of the crime. Here is an iron clad axiom that could not be more imbecilic. *In atrocissimis leviores coniecturiae sufficiunt, et licet iudici iura transgredi.* Let us translate this into ordinary words so that all Europeans can understand one of the many equally stupid reasons given them by those who know nothing of the subject. *In the most atrocious crimes, that is, the rarest, the slightest conjectures are sufficient and it is lawful for the judge to go beyond the law.* The practical absurdities in legislation are frequently the products of fear which is the main source of human conflict. The legislators (or rather the lawyers, by chance authorized as experts who decided on all things when they were alive, then later having written decisions according to their own venal interests, becoming arbiters and legislators of the fortunes of men), frightened by the condemnation of some innocent man, loaded up jurisprudence with excessive formalities and exceptions, the strict observance of which would with impunity seat anarchy on the throne of justice. Frightened by other atrocious crimes that were difficult to prove, they believed it was necessary to override this same formality they had established, so now with impatient despotism and with ladylike trepidation they transformed serious judicial decision making into a kind of betting game with hazard and trickery as its principle players.]]

men will lie because it is easier for men to be overcome by illusions fed by ignorance or by hate of an oppressor claiming to exercise the power of God who has not given it to him, indeed has taken it away from all those He created.[2] In the case of wanton cruelty, man is not merciless in excess of his own interests, hate or fear that he imagines. There is really no excess sentiment in man; it is always proportional to how he perceives the facts. Similarly, the credibility of a witness may be diminished sometimes when he is a member of a secret society which has its own customs that are poorly understood, and has interests that are different from the public. Such a man not only has his own passions but those of the secret society as well.

Finally, a witness has almost no credibility when the crime consists of words.[3] The tenor, the gesticulations, everything which precedes and follows the different ideas which men attach to the same words, alter and modify every statement, so that a witness will find it impossible to comprehend exactly what was said. Moreover, violent actions are so much outside ordinary experience that the crimes leave traces of their effects in a multitude of circumstances, but the words remain only in the memory of the listeners whose memory may be unreliable and often deceived. Thus it is much easier to prove guilt through the calumny of words than through the assessment of actions, because the greater the number of circumstances called as evidence, the greater are the chances of the accused to exculpate himself.

§ XIV. [Evidence and Forms of Judgment

A useful approach for deciding whether a crime was committed requires that one assess the weight of the evidence. When the proofs of a fact are dependent on each other they cannot themselves either increase or decrease the probability that a crime occurred, since evidence lacking in antecedent proofs will also affect subsequent ones. [[Furthermore, proofs derived from a single fact are all equally dependent on that single fact so increasing the number of proofs cannot increase the reliability of the evidence.]] Thus, when proofs are completely independent of each other the evidence produced gains in weight in accordance with the proofs provided, because the invalidation of one piece of evidence does not invalidate any other. I speak here of the material probability of crimes, the evidence for which, because they merit punishment, must be completely certain. But this paradox disappears when one considers that, strictly speaking, moral certainty can only reflect a probability, even though it is commonly equated with certainty; every man of good sense agrees to this custom which is born of the need to act decisively. Thus, the certainty required to assess the guilt of any man drives the more important activities of everyday life. As such, it supersedes all speculation. [[We may distinguish two types of proofs of guilt, perfect and imperfect. I call perfect proofs those that exclude the possibility that a man is innocent; I call imperfect those that do not exclude this possibility. Of the first, just one proof is sufficient for the finding of guilt; of the second as many proofs as are needed for a perfect proof, given that each of these separately is not sufficient, but are so when all are combined. It should be noted that an imperfect proof of which a man may clear himself and does not do so, becomes a perfect proof. But this moral certainty is easier to feel than to define.]] Therefore I believe that the best law is that which does not assign jurors chosen by the principal judge, but rather assigns jurors chosen by lot, because in this case ignorance guided by sentiment is much better than science dominated by judicial opinion. Where the laws are clear and precise the office of the judge needs simply to ascertain the facts. If, in search for proofs of a crime, ability and

37

adroitness are required; or if, in presenting the verdict clarity and precision are necessary, the judge will find the answer in simple and ordinary common sense, not in the fallacies of "wisdom" to which the judge is habituated and which reduces everything to an artificial system based on the legal theory he has previously studied. Happy is the nation where law is not reduced to a science![1] The most useful laws are those where every man is judged by his peers, where justice is forged by liberty and for the good of all citizens, which means that it is affected equally by the sentiments of the lower and upper classes: whether the contempt with which the lower classes regard the upper classes or vice versa. When the crime inflicts injury on another citizen, then half the jurors must be peers of the accused, the other half those of the victim; thus weighing the balance of private interests that may taint the facts against the supposed truth spoken by the law. It is also just for the accused to exclude as jurors those who suspect him, and therefore, other things being equal, after a period of time he may appear to convict himself. Let verdicts and proofs of guilt be made public so that public opinion, which is perhaps the only source of societal bonding, acts as a brake on powerful human passions. The people say, "we are not slaves and we are not defenseless," a courageous sentiment and an inspiration to the sovereign who knows his own interests. I will not add any further details and cautions required by such institutions. What I have said is clear enough. It should not be necessary for me to say anything else.]

§ XV. Secret Accusations

The hallowed mess of secret accusations is manifest in many nations[1] whose weak government makes them a necessity. This custom makes men furtive and deceitful. Anyone who suspects another turns him into an enemy. Thus, as men habitually hide their feelings from others, they end up hiding them from themselves, and so they become devoid of true sentiments. Men are so unhappy when they are without clear and solid principles to guide them; lost and rudderless in the vast sea of public opinion, constantly preoccupied with protecting themselves from monsters that threaten them, living every moment embittered by an uncertain future. Deprived of the lasting satisfaction offered by tranquility and security, they hastily grasp at fleeting moments of comfort from their disordered, pathetic lives, hoping that this justifies their existence. Can we turn these men into intrepid soldiers, defenders of their country or throne? And will we find among them incorruptible judges who, with the spirit of liberty and eloquent patriotism, foster and enrich the true interests of the sovereign; who bring to the throne tributes of love and benediction from men of all rank, and by this render to palaces and cottages alike peace, security, industry and hope for a better future, a useful agitation for the life of states?

Who is able to defend against calumny when it is protected by *secrecy*, the strongest shield of tyranny? What kind of government is it when he who rules suspects everyone as his enemy, and feels compelled, in order to establish public tranquility, to take it away from everyone?

[What are the real justifications for secret accusations and punishments—the public welfare, the security and maintenance of the form of government? But what kind of strange government is it when, with both force and popular opinion on its side, it fears every citizen? Or is it to protect the identity of the accuser? Then the laws are insufficient to protect him, in which case there would be subjects who were more powerful than the sovereign! Is it because of the shame felt by the informer? Then this would authorize secret calumnies and punish them only when public! Is it the nature of the crime? If everyday actions, even those useful to the public are called crimes, then accusations and trials can never be secret enough. Is it not in everyone's interest that any crimes against the public good should be publicized as an example? I respect all governments, and I do not speak here of any one in particular, when I say that there are some circumstances in which unbridled treachery is so embedded in the government that one would have to destroy it in order to save the nation. But if I were asked to do so even in some lost corner of the universe, I would make the necessary laws only with a trembling hand, mindful of the gaze of future generations.] I have already referred to Montesquieu who argued that public accusations were more compatible with a republic, where the public good is the primary passion of all citizens; unlike a monarchy where this sentiment is very weak because of its form of government, where it is kept stable by appointed commissioners who in the name of the public make accusations against those who break the law. But every government, whether republic or monarchy, should punish false accusers as much as it does the accused.

§ XVI. Torture

A cruelty consecrated by its use in the majority of nations is torture of the accused while his trial is in progress. Its purpose is to force the accused to confess a crime by eliciting contradictions in his testimony, by identifying accomplices, by purging infamy through I know not what metaphysics and incomprehensible methods, [or finally by uncovering crimes that he may have committed but for which he was not charged].

Only a judge can pronounce a man *guilty* of a crime. Nor can society deprive the accused of public protection if he has not violated the social contract. What is it about the law, if it is not force, that gives the judge the power to apply a punishment to a citizen, while there remains doubt as to his guilt or innocence? This is a familiar dilemma: either it is certain or not certain that a crime has been committed. If certain, then other punishments that detract from the stability of the laws are useless torments because getting a confession from the accused is unnecessary. If uncertain, an accused person should not be tormented because he is, according to the law, presumed innocent until proved guilty. But I would add that the ultimate confusion arises when a tortured man becomes both accuser and accused at the same time; when pain becomes the crucible of truth, as though it resides in the very muscles and nerves of his miserable body. This is a sure method to absolve the robust wicked and condemn the innocent weak.[1] Behold the inconvenient flaws in this pretense to truth, worthy of cannibals, reminiscent of the way the Romans treated their slaves—all the time admired even though they were barbarians and victims of their own fierce and excessively glorified virtue.

What is the political purpose of punishment? To terrorize other men. But what kind of justice must result from secret and private slaughter, a tyranny applied equally to both the guilty and the innocent? It is of course important that no crime should go unpunished, but it is useless to identify who committed a crime that has been long buried in darkness. A crime already committed, which by definition cannot be rectified, should be punished by political society only with the intent to deter others from committing the same crime.[2] If it is true that many more men, whether because they are timid or virtuous, respect the laws than those who break them, the risk of tormenting innocent people must be so much the greater.

Another ridiculous reason for torture is the purgation of infamy, that is, a man judged guilty of infamy must confirm this by having his bones torn apart. This abuse must not be tolerated in the eighteenth century. It is believed that pain, which is a sensation, purges infamy and that this reflects a simple moral relationship. Doesn't it follow that infamy is an impure mixture of sentiments, including morality? Perhaps pain is its crucible? It is not difficult to recount the origin of this ridiculous law, because the same absurdities adopted within one nation have always had some relationship to other common ideas that have come to be respected. It seems that the custom has been taken from religious or spiritual ideas that have had considerable influence on the thoughts of men, on nations and even centuries. An infallible dogma assures us the stains of sin result from human weakness and that, so as not to invite the eternal anger of the Great Being, they must be eradicated—incomprehensibly—by fire.[3] Now since pain and fire remove the stains of spirit and of personal guilt, why cannot the agony of torture remove the civil stain of infamy? I believe that the confession of the accused, which in some jurisdictions is seen as essential for a verdict, has similar origins because in the mysterious trial of penance the confession of sins is an essential part of the sacrament. Behold how men abuse the reassuring light of Revelation which is all they have to comfort them in times of ignorance, when, through human weakness they make absurd and far fetched applications to every situation. But infamy is a sentiment not subject to law or reason, but to common opinion. Torture similarly induces acts of infamy against innocent victims. So infamy causes infamy.

The third purpose of torture is to uncover contradictions in the offender's testimony, as though the fear of punishment, uncertainty of the trial, the apparatus and majesty of the court, the common ignorance of both the guilty and the innocent, were not enough to reveal contradictions among the innocent who are afraid, and among the guilty who are trying to conceal their deeds. Contradictions are common enough among men in times of tranquility, but are multiplied many times when the mind is absorbed with thoughts of escape from imminent peril.

This infamous crucible of truth is a monument to the continuation of ancient and barbarous procedures when guilt was established through the *judgment* of God, the ordeals of fire, boiling water and the fate of armed combat—as though the links of the eternal chain that originates from the First cause could be disordered and disconnected at every moment by these frivolous human practices.[4] The only difference between torture and trial by fire and boiling water is that the first depends on the willingness of the accused to speak, and the second on facts purely physical and extraneous to the individual. But this difference is apparent and not real. This is because there is little freedom to speak the truth during the applications of torture especially as fire and boiling water do not prevent telling lies. Every one of our willful acts is always proportionate to the amount felt by our senses, which are not infinite; indeed the sensitivity of every man is limited. Thus the impression of pain expands to a point that it completely occupies the mind clamoring to free itself from torture; so at every moment a person will choose the easiest way out from pain. Therefore the response of the accused is necessarily in proportion to his sensations of fire and boiling water. An innocent man who is sensitive will plead guilty when he believes that it will put a stop to his torture. In this way, every difference between the guilty and the innocent vanishes by utilizing the very means allegedly used to ascertain it.

[It is unnecessary to recount the innumerable shining examples of innocents who confessed their guilt under the agony of torture: there is no nation, no age that does not provide them. Yet men do not change, nor do they draw the necessary conclusions from these examples. There is no man, having thought hard beyond the basic necessities of life, who on occasion is drawn to nature, calling him with her secret and confusing voices. But custom, the tyranny of the minds, pulls him back and frightens him.] The effect of torture therefore is a matter of temperament and of calculation, which varies for every man in proportion to his inner strength and his sensibility. A mathematician could solve this problem better than a judge: given the innocent's physical strength and the sensibility of his every nerve, the judge must find the correct proportion of pain needed to obtain a confession of a given crime.

The accused is examined in order to find the truth. But if this elusive truth is hard to find somewhere in the air, a gesture, or the physiognomy of a calm individual, it will be much harder to discover in an individual who is convulsed with pain along with the usual signs that most individuals display when questioned. These signs by which we distinguish between truth and falsity are vanquished by the very violent action which confounds them.

These truths were known to the Roman legislators because they did not use torture except on slaves who lacked the legal status of persons. Torture is not used in England,[5] a nation in which the glory of literature, the superiority of commerce and of wealth, reflects its greatness. Their examples of virtue and courage leave no doubt about the goodness of their laws. Torture was abolished in Sweden[6] and also by one of the wisest of Europe's monarchs[7] who, importing philosophy into his reign, brought about friendly legislation to his subjects by putting equality and freedom back into the laws, which is the only kind of equality and liberty that men can reasonably wish to have in the present circumstances. Torture is considered unnecessary even in the law of armies, which are for the most part made up of the dregs of nations, and would therefore use it more than any other group.

How strange, when one considers how great is this tyrannical custom, that the laws of peace must learn a more human approach to criminal justice from minds hardened by butchery and blood! This truth is finally heard, although muddled, by such people not so far away. They say that the confession is not just, if it is made under torture, but is not confirmed by an oath after the torture has stopped; and if the accused does not confirm the crime then he must be tortured again. Some doctors and some nations do not permit this abominable principle to be applied more than three times. Other nations and other doctors leave it to the arbitrary decision of the judge. This means that where two men are equally innocent or equally guilty, then the strongest and most brave will be absolved, the weak and timid condemned in accordance with this rationale: *I, the judge must find you the accused guilty of such and such a crime; you have vigorously resisted pain and therefore I will absolve you; being weak, you have confessed, therefore I condemn you. I feel that the confession torn from you during the torments carries little weight, but I will torment you anew if you do not confirm the confession you have made.*

A strange consequence that necessarily follows from this use of torture is that the innocent man is placed in a worse position than the guilty. This is because if both of them receive torture, the innocent suffers all the negative consequences because he either confesses the crime and is condemned or is declared innocent but has still suffered the punishment.[8] But the guilty has a more favorable case because if he resists the torture without it stopping, he must be declared innocent and so has exchanged a greater punishment for a lesser one. And so the innocent must lose and the guilty wins.

A law that commands torture is a law that says: *Men, resist pain, and if nature has blessed you with an unquenchable true love of yourselves, if you have given an unassailable legal defense, I create in you a completely different emotion, which is an heroic hatred of yourselves, and*

I command you to accuse yourselves, speaking the truth in between the ripping of your muscles and the tearing apart of your bones.

[If torture is used to uncover other crimes for which the guilty individual has not been charged, this is its rationale: *You are guilty of one crime, well then it is possible that you are guilty of a hundred other crimes; doubt about this weighs on me, so I wish to make sure it is true; the laws torment you because you are guilty, because you are able to be guilty, and because I want you to be guilty.*]

Finally, torture is used to make the offender reveal his accomplices. But if it is shown that it cannot uncover even the most basic truth, how is it able to reveal the accomplices when they are part of that truth? It is as if a man can more easily accuse his accomplices than himself. Is it right to torment a man because of the crimes of others? Cannot accomplices be discovered through examination of testimony, examination of the accused, from proofs and from the material facts of the crime, in sum from all those same factors that must be used to ascertain the crime of the accused? Accomplices usually flee immediately after their companion is incarcerated; their uncertain lot condemns them to lonely exile and frees the nation from the danger of new offenses. Meanwhile the punishment of the guilty in custody achieves its proper end which is to deter through terror other men from doing the same crime.[9]

§ XVII. [[Revenue Authorities[1]

There was a time when almost all punishments were pecuniary.[2] Dealing with crimes was the province of the prince. Attacks against public security were an opportunity for gain, so whoever was designated to defend public security had an interest in finding an offence against it. The object of punishment was then a matter of litigation between the revenue authority (the administrator of this punishment) and the accused: a civil affair, contentious, private rather than public. It gave to the revenue authority other rights that these bureaucrats defended on behalf of the public and gave to the accused other wrongs with which to strike him down as a necessary example. The judge was therefore an advocate of the revenue authority rather than a detached inquirer of the truth; an agent of the treasury instead of the protector and the minister of the laws. But whereas in this system the confessions of the offender were confessions of debt owed to the revenue authority, the purpose was the same as in the criminal procedure: to obtain a confession framed so as to favor the interest of the revenue authority, which became and still is the center of all criminal law machinery (since the effects always continue very long after the causes). Without this confession an accused convicted by indubitable proofs will receive less than the prescribed punishment; without the confession he will not suffer torture beyond those prescribed for the same kinds of crimes that he could have committed. With this confession the judge takes complete possession of the offender and mangles him with methodical formality, in order to dig deep inside him, as from an acquired property to get everything from which he may profit. By proving the existence of a crime, the confession offers a convincing proof and makes this proof seem less suspect through the agony and desperation from intense pain that accompanies it—in contrast to an extra-judicial confession that is taken calmly, with detachment, without the fears of judicial torment, which is not enough for condemnation. Investigations and proofs that uncover the facts that go against the interests of the treasury are excluded. It is not out of concern for misery and weakness of the offender that he is sometimes saved from torture, but out of concern for

47

losses that his authority might suffer, which is nowadays imaginary and inconceivable. The judge becomes the enemy of the offender, of a man in manacles, given as wretched booty, to torments becoming more and more terrible; not looking for the truth of fact, but looking for the crime in the prisoner. If he cannot succeed through this trickery, he believes he will lose, making a dent in that infallibility which such men arrogate to themselves in all things.

The incriminating clues are in the power of the judge; because for one to be proved innocent one must first be found guilty: this is called an *offensive proceeding,*[3] and it is found in the criminal procedures of every part of enlightened Europe in the eighteenth century. The true process, the *informative proceeding*, investigates the facts differently with reason in command, an approach adopted in military law, even used by Asian despots in neutral and unexceptional cases, but rarely used in European tribunals. What a complicated labyrinth of strange absurdities, which a happier posterity will surely find incredible! Only philosophers of that time could confirm that the nature of man was capable of producing such a system.]]

§ XVIII. Oaths

A contradiction between the law and natural human sentiments arises when oaths are demanded of the accused in order to make him speak the truth, when his greatest interest is to lie. It is as though a man should swear to the truth in order to bring about his own destruction. As though religion when it should speak in the interest of men, remains silent. The experience of each century has shown that men have more and more abused this precious gift from heaven. So why should the wicked respect it if those deemed the wisest of men frequently violate it? For most men the motives that religion imposes on the tumult of fear and on the love of life are too weak because they are too far removed from senses. The affairs of heaven are regulated by laws very different from those that regulate the affairs of men. Why should one compromise the other? Why put man in a terrible contradiction between losing God, or colluding in his own ruin? The laws requiring him to take an oath force him either to be an evil Christian or a martyr. The oath becomes little by little a simple formality, as it destroys the power of religious sentiment that forms the unique basis of the honesty of the greater number of men. Experience shows how useless these oaths are, for any judge can testify that an oath has never made the accused speak the truth. Reason makes us see this, showing clearly the futility and damaging consequences of all laws that go against the natural sentiments of men. Their destiny is like that of dikes put across a river to change its course: they either give way and are immediately broken through, or the currents form a vortex that slowly erodes them.

§ XIX. Prompt Punishment

The more prompt and closer the punishment is to the crime, the more just and useful it will be. I say more just because it saves the offender the useless and cruel torment of uncertainty that grows in a vigorous imagination and weakens his sentiment. More just because the deprivation of liberty is itself a punishment and should not precede the sentence except where absolutely necessary. The prison is then the simple confinement of a citizen until he is judged guilty, and this confinement, being essentially punitive, must be as short as possible and must be of the least possible severity. The minimal duration should be determined by the necessary time needed for the trial and the right of those who have been detained the longest to be tried first. The severity of the confinement must be only that necessary either to prevent escape or to prevent the hiding of proofs of the crime. The trial must be finished in as brief a time as possible. What more disgusting contrast than the laziness of a judge and the anguish of the accused? The comforts and pleasures of an insensitive judge on one side and on the other the tears and squalor of the accused? In general, the burden of a punishment and the consequence of a crime must be directed to others, all the while inflicting the least possible hardship on those who suffer it, because one cannot regard a society as legitimate that does not hold to the infallible principle that its citizens should wish to be subjected to the least evil possible.[1]

I have said that the promptness of punishment is more efficient because the shorter the time between the punishment and the misdeed, the stronger and more lasting will be the association in the human mind of the two ideas—*crime and punishment*—such that one is felt as cause and the other as the necessary and inevitable effect. It has been demonstrated that the association of ideas is the cement that binds the entire fabric of human intellect, without which pleasure and pain would be isolated sensations of no import.[2] The more men are separated from these general ideas and these universal principles, the more they become vulgar, and the more they live only for the present and immediate associations, ignoring the more distant and complicated ones that are useful only to men strongly

51

impassioned for the object to which they are inclined. Thus the light of their attention is focused only on this single object, leaving all others in darkness. Those with more elevated minds have developed the habit of assimilating many objects at the same time and have the facility to contrast many partial sensations with others with the result that their actions are less dangerous and more predictable.[3]

The close proximity of the punishment to the crime is therefore of supreme importance. If a rough and ready vulgar mind is seduced by the picture of an advantageous crime, it immediately sees the risk in doing it because it is associated with the idea of punishment. A long delay will produce no other effect than to further split the two ideas and, although the punishment of the crime does make an impression [which is more effective as a spectacle than as a punishment] such impression takes effect only when the horror of a particular crime, which would reinforce the feeling of punishment in the minds of the spectators, has weakened.

Another principle that seems admirably to strengthen even more the important link between the misdeed and the punishment is that it should reflect as much as possible the nature of the crime.[4] This analogy wonderfully facilitates the contrast that must be made between the force of the crime and the repercussions of the punishment. That is, it leads the mind in the opposite direction to the one toward which the seductive idea of breaking the law is aimed.

§ XX. Violent Crimes

Some crimes are committed against the person, others against property. The former must be unerringly punished with corporal punishment[1]: neither the grand nor rich should be able to put a price on their assaults against the weak or impoverished[2]; otherwise the riches that, under the eye of the law are the reward of the industry, will feed tyranny. There is no liberty when the laws at any time permit a situation where a man who should be treated as a *person* then becomes a *thing*. Then you will see how the energy of the powerful extracts out of the many combinations of social relationships the ones that, under the law, are in their favor. This discovery is the magical secret that turns citizens into beasts of burden; it is the chain in the hand of the strong which binds the actions of the unwary and the weak. This is the reason why, in some governments that have all the appearance of liberty, tyranny lies hidden or introduces itself unforeseen into some corner neglected by the legislator, where it imperceptibly gains strength and grows. Men mostly make very solid stands against overt tyranny, but they do not see the imperceptible insect which gnaws them and opens a door (more secure because it is concealed) for the river's flood.

§ XXI. [Punishing Nobles

What then should be the punishment for the crimes of nobles, the privileged who shape a large part of the laws of nations?[1] I will not here examine whether this hereditary distinction between nobles and commoners is useful for a government or necessary for a monarchy, whether it is true that it forms an intermediary power which limits the excesses of the two extremes;[2] whether it makes up a rank that is a slave to itself and to others and keeps the entire circulation of reputation and hope within an impenetrable circle just like the fertile and luscious oases that spring up in the vast sandy deserts of Arabia. Nor shall I examine whether it is true that inequality is inevitable or useful in society, or that this inequality should exist among social classes rather than among individuals, or should be limited to one portion of society rather than circulating throughout the political body, or perpetuating itself instead of being continuously renewed and self-destroyed.[3]

I will restrict myself only to the punishment appropriate to this class asserting that it must be the same for the highest to the lowest citizen. Every legitimate distinction whether in honor or wealth presupposes an anterior equality founded on the law, on which all subjects are equally dependent. One must suppose that men who have renounced their natural inclination to despotism have said: *He who is more industrious will have greater honors, and his fame will reflect on his descendants; but if he who is happier or more honored hopes for more he must not violate the social compacts which elevate him above others. It is true that such decrees were never issued from an assembly of humankind,[4] but they exist in the immutable relationships of things; they do not undermine those advantages supposedly produced by the nobility and prevent their inconveniences; they make strong laws that close off the paths to impunity of the privileged.* It is said that giving the same punishment to nobles and commoners is not really the same because of the difference in education and the additional dishonor that is cast on an illustrious family. To which I respond that the sensibility of the criminal is not a measure of the punishment, but rather it is the damage to the public—which is greater

55

when committed by a person of rank. And that the equality of punishment can only be extrinsic, since its intrinsic effects are very diverse in every individual, and that the sovereign should neutralize the dishonor of the criminal's family by a public demonstration of benevolence towards the innocent family. And who does not understand that sensibilities take the place of reason in an incredulous and admiring public?]

§ XXII. Theft

Theft that is not accompanied by violence should receive a monetary punishment. He who lines his own pockets at the expense of others must be made poor.[1] But this is usually a crime of misery and desperation, a crime of this unhappy part of men to whom the right of property (terrible, and perhaps an unnecessary right)[2] has left them a meager existence. [Furthermore the monetary punishment increases the number of offenders to a level higher than the crime itself because it takes away the bread of the innocent[3] by taking it away from the guilty.] A more appropriate punishment for this crime would be the only kind of servitude that can be considered just, that is the temporary enslavement to society of the labor and the person of the offender,[4] a repayment with a true and perfect dependence on the unjust despotism with which the offender has usurped the social contract.

But when the theft is committed with violence, the punishment must also include corporal punishment and servitude.[5] Other writers before me have demonstrated the inevitable disorder that arises when there has been no clear distinction between punishments for theft with violence and fraudulent thefts, by making an absurd equation of a gross sum of money with the life of a man. But it is never superfluous to repeat this equation which has almost never been put into practice. The political machinery, more than any other, clings to its conceptual framework and is very slow to take on new ideas. These are crimes of a different nature, and the mathematical axiom which states that infinity separates heterogeneous quantities can most certainly be applied even in politics.[6]

§ XXIII. Public Condemnation

Personal injuries against honor, that is against the correct amount of esteem that a citizen has the right to expect from others, must be punished with public condemnation.[1] This condemnation is a signal of public disapproval that deprives the offender of public acceptance, of the trust of his country and of the brotherhood that is the inspiration of society. This is not a matter of legal discretion. It is therefore necessary that the condemnation inflicted by the law should be the same that emanates from the relationship of things, the same as that which comes from universal morality or from a specific morality deriving from particular systems that inspire common opinion in a given nation. If the one is different from the other, either the law loses public veneration, or the ideas of morality and probity vanish, despite declamations which can never overcome the weight of examples. If we declare indifferent actions as infamous, then this diminishes the infamy of actions that are truly so. The punishment of infamy[2] must not be too frequent or fall upon a great number of persons in any one time: Not the first, because the real impressions on opinion of things that are too often repeated weaken that same opinion; not the latter because the infamy of many dissolves into the infamy of none.

[[Corporal punishments and grief must not be given for these crimes, which, founded on conceit, derive glory and nourishment from that same grief. More suitable are ridicule and condemnation, punishments that break down the conceit of fanatics using the conceit of spectators,[3] from whose tenacity truth can only break free with slow and obstinate force. The smart legislator, using force against force, opinion against opinion breaks down the admiration and wonder of the common people who are given of a false principle, and uses the correctly deduced consequences of the principle to hide from them its original absurdity.]]

This is how to avoid confusing relationships and the invariable nature of things, which, not limited by time and going on incessantly, challenges and unravels all the limits of regulation when they turn away from its course. Not only do the arts of taste and pleasure faithfully imitate the universal principle of nature, but politics itself, at least when true and permanent, is subject to this general maxim. For it is none other than the art of better controlling and rendering together the immutable sentiments of men.

§ XXIV. Political Indolence

Whoever disturbs the public peace, who does not obey the laws which are the conditions by which men mutually abide and defend themselves, must be excluded from society, that is, must be banished. This is the reason why a wise government will not suffer political indolence in its midst of labor and industry. This kind of political idleness has been confused by stern moralists with the laziness of the rich who accumulate capital from industry, which is both necessary and useful, insofar as society expands and administration becomes centralized. I call political indolence[1] that which contributes nothing to society either through labor or wealth, which is acquired without ever risking its loss. It is venerated by common people with stupid admiration, and looked upon by the wise with scornful compassion for the beings who are its victims. The political indolent, lacking the stimulus toward an active existence that is essential to preserve and increase the comforts of life, put all their energy into the passion of opinions, which are by no means the less strong ones. A person who enjoys the fruits of vices and virtue of his own ancestors is not politically indolent. Nor is one who enjoys selling the bread of existence for his temporary pleasure to the hard working poor, who peacefully capitalized on the hidden war within industry, instead of employing uncertainty and bloody force. Thus, it is not for the austerity and limited virtue of some censors to define what indolence should be punished, but for the law.

[[It seems that banishment must be given to those accused of an atrocious crime, who are very likely but not certain to be guilty. But if this is to be done it is necessary for a law to be less arbitrary yet as precise as possible. However, banishment of the condemned forces the nation to make a fateful choice between either fearing them or hurting them, while nevertheless leaving them the sacred right to prove their innocence. There must be stronger reasons to banish a citizen than being a foreigner; stronger reasons to banish a first time offender than being a recidivist.]]

§ XXV. Banishment and Confiscation

But should a member of society who has been forever banished and excluded be deprived of his worldly possessions? This question can be interpreted in different ways. Losing one's possessions is a punishment more severe than banishment; there must be some cases in which, in proportion to the crime, everything or a part of one's possessions should be taken, and some where none at all should be taken. The loss of everything will occur when banishment is ordered by law, an action which eradicates all relationships between society and the delinquent citizen; a case of living death for the citizen, and as far as the body politic is concerned, it must produce the same effect as actual death. It would seem then that all his possessions should be passed on to his legitimate heirs rather than to the sovereign because banishment is the same as death in respect to the body politic. But it is not for this nicety that I dare to disapprove of the confiscation of worldly possessions. If as some have claimed, confiscation impedes vendettas and stops bullying, they have not considered that, however much good punishment produces, it does not follow that it is always just, for to be so it must always be necessary. Nor can a useful injustice be tolerated by a legislator who wants to close all doors to a vigilant tyranny that allures with temporary benefits and the happiness of a few illustrious persons, all the time disdainful of the future extermination and the tears of the forgotten masses. Confiscation puts a price on the heads of the weak, makes the innocent suffer the punishment of a criminal and places those same innocents in the desperate situation of having to commit crimes. What sadder spectacle than a family overwhelmed by dishonor and misery by the crimes of the head of their household, made powerless by the law of submission[1] which forbids its members from preventing such crimes, even if there were a way to do so?

§ XXVI. On the Spirit of the Family

Dire and official injustices have been approved by men even of high standing, and applied in the more liberal republics, because they think of society as a union of families rather than a union of men. Suppose there are one hundred thousand men or twenty thousand families each of which is composed of five persons, with the head of the family as its representative: If society is computed according to families, there will be twenty thousand men and eighty thousand slaves; if computed according to men, there will be one hundred thousand citizens and no slaves. In the first case there will be a republic composed of twenty thousand little monarchies; in the second case the republican spirit will not only be expressed in the town squares and in gatherings of nations, but also inside the citizens' homes where the greater part of happiness and misery of men resides. In the first case, the laws and customs are the result of the habitual sentiments of members of the republic, who are the heads of each family: the spirit of monarchy would be introduced little by little into that same republic, whose effects would be held back only by the opposing interests of each family, not once displaying the spirit of liberty and equality. The spirit of the family is a spirit of particulars and picayune facts. When the spirit is fostered by the republic of men, its patron is general principles; the republic comprehends the facts and condenses them into categories of important principles that are good for the greater majority of its citizens. In a republic of families, the sons remain under the power of the head of the family while he is still alive, and are forced to wait until his death in order to be allowed to have an existence dependent solely on laws.[1] Being accustomed to buckling under and fearing (the father) at a verdant and vigorous age, when the sentiments are less influenced by fear based on experience, which is called moderation, how can they overcome the obstacles posed by the perennial opposition of vice over virtue, and in their languid and declining years, when any vigorous reform is counteracted by their despair of seeing the results?

When there is a republic of men, the family is not subordinated by a command, but by a contract, and the sons, at an age when they are dependent on nature—frail, lacking education and means of defense—become free members of the city, and are only subordinate to the head of the family through sharing in the advantages available to all free men in the great society. In the first case the sons, that is the majority and most useful members of a nation, are subject to the discretion of the fathers; in the second case there is no other arm of command beyond this sacred and inviolable form of organization that reciprocally provides for basic needs, and this in gratitude for benefits received, which is undermined not so much by evils of the human heart, but by subjection to a poor interpretation of the purpose of law.

Such contradictions between family bonds and the foundation of the republic are a fertile source of other contradictions between domestic and public morality, and therefore give rise to perpetual conflict in the mind of every man.[2] In the first case it inspires submission and fear; the second case courage and liberty. In the former man learns to confine his beneficence to a small number of people whom he did not choose, the latter extends beneficence to all classes of men. The first constantly demands a personal sacrifice to a vain idol, which is called *good of the family*, which is often times not for the good of any member of the family, and the second teaches men to seek personal advantage without offending the laws, or incites self sacrifice to a fanatical patriotism which fosters action. Such contradictions make men disdain virtue which they find impenetrable and confused, and so distant that even physical and moral objects are obscured. How many times, in remembering past actions, is man astonished to find dishonesty! As a society grows larger the significance of each member becomes less and the republican sentiment is diminished if the citizen is not protected by the laws. Societies have, like human bodies, circumscribed limits to their growth, and the economy is necessarily upset should they grow beyond these limits. It seems that the size of one state must be the inverse of the sensibility of its members, otherwise, as they both grow, the good laws will be obstructed from preventing crime by the good they themselves have produced. A republic that is too large cannot save citizens from despotism unless it subdivides itself and then reunifies as numerous federal republics. But how is this to be achieved? From a despotic dictator who has the courage of Silla[3] and the genius to build as well as to destroy. For the man who would be ambitious the glory of all the centuries awaits him; he who would be a philosopher, the gratitude of all his citizens will console him in the loss of his authority, right at the time when he may become indifferent to them.

As our sentiments combine to unify a nation they become weaker so the feeling toward objects that are closer to us grows stronger; therefore under stronger despotism personal friendships are more lasting, and the virtue of the family that has always taken second place is the most common, indeed is the only virtue. Thus it is easy to see how limited have been the perspectives of most legislators.

§ XXVII. The Mildness of Punishments

But this line of thinking has taken me away from my subject, to the clarification of which I hasten to return. One of the best deterrents of crime is not the cruelty of punishment, but its certainty.[1] Thus, for it to be a useful virtue, punishment requires the vigilance and severity of inexorable judges to be accompanied by mild legislation. The certainty of a well moderated punishment will always make a greater impression than the fear of a more severe punishment that is accompanied by the hope of impunity. This is because even the least evils, when they are certain, constantly scare the human mind; and hope, a gift from heaven on which we pin everything, always removes from us the idea of worse evils, especially when the hope of impunity is enhanced by avarice and weakness.[2] Severe punishment itself promotes the evil that it opposes by daring men to take even greater risks; it causes them to commit more crimes to escape the punishment of one. In different countries and times of severe punishments they have always been those of most bloody and inhuman acts, because that same ferocious spirit guided the hand of the legislator, as it did parricides and assassins. The throne dictated laws of iron for the savage minds of slaves to obey. In private darkness they encouraged the destruction of one tyrant to make room for another.

As punishments become more cruel, so the minds of men, like fluids that always adjust their level according to the objects around them, become more callous; always nourished by the passions. After a hundred years of cruel punishments, the wheel[3] frightens no more than prison previously did. This is because one punishment obtains sufficient effect when its severity just exceeds the benefit the offender receives from the crime, and the degree of excess must be calculated precisely according to the damage to public good caused by the crime. Any additional punishment is superfluous and therefore a tyranny. Men are regulated through the repeated effects of evils that they know, not through those that they do not know. Consider two nations in which the scale of punishment is proportioned to the scale of crimes, one where the severest punishment is perpetual slavery, the other the wheel. I say that the first would engender no greater fear of its severest punishment than the second;[4] and if there were a reason for the first of these nations to adopt the more severe punishment of the second, the same rationale would serve to increase the punishment of the last, trading insensibility to the torments of the wheel for a slower and more studied punishment, and right up to the refinements of a "science" too well known by tyrants.

Two other pernicious consequences follow from the cruelty of punishment that works against the very purpose of preventing crime.[5] The first is that it is not easy to establish the exact proportion between the crime and the punishment because, however much an industrious cruelty produces a great variety of punishments, it is not possible to go beyond the ultimate force which limits human organization and sensibility.[6] Allied to this is that, at the extreme it is not possible to find a crime more damaging and the corresponding more severe punishment that would be necessary in order to prevent it. The second consequence is the impunity that arises from the cruelty of punishments. Men are contained within certain limits, both for good and for evil and a spectacle of excessive cruelty for humanity can be nothing other than a passing rage, but never an enduring system which laws must be. If the laws are really cruel, unless they are changed, fatal impunity will be born of those same laws. Who has not read stories and been horrified by savage and useless torments which were coldly invented and conducted by men who were deemed wise?

Who cannot help but tremble at seeing thousands of wretches whose misery, willed or tolerated by the laws that have always favored the few and violated the many, forces them in desperation to return to the original state of nature; or seeing them accused of impossible crimes fabricated by fearful ignorance, found guilty only of being faithful to their own principles by men endowed with those same senses, and as a consequence of those passions, with thoughtful formality and slow lacerations of torture, a spectacular game of a fanatical multitude ensues.[7]

§ XXVIII. The Punishment of Death

Concerning this useless extravagance of punishments, which has never improved men's lives, I am forced to ask whether the death penalty is truly useful and just in a well organized government. What gives men the right to kill other men? It certainly does not follow from the right from which sovereignty and law derive. These result from the sum of the small portions of private liberty of each person given up for the common good; they represent the general will which is the aggregation of individual wills.[1] Who has ever wanted to give the right to other men to decide to kill another? How can the smallest sacrifice of liberty of each person ever amount to the greatest of all good, a life? And even if it did, how does it comport with the other principle that a man may not kill himself, and so how is he able to give this right to others or even to the whole of society?

The punishment of death then is not a *right*. In fact I have demonstrated that such a right amounts to nothing but a war of a nation against a citizen whom it judges necessary and useful to destroy. But if I can demonstrate that death is neither useful nor necessary, I will have won the cause of humanity. The death of a citizen cannot be considered necessary except for two reasons. First, even when deprived of liberty the citizen still has relationships and power that may concern the security of the nation; since his very existence could produce a dangerous revolution in a stable form of government.

The death of this citizen therefore becomes a necessity when a nation is recovering or has lost its liberty, or in a time of anarchy, when disorder takes the place of law. But during tranquil rule of law in a form of government generally supported by the voters and when it is well fortified both outside and inside by force and by opinion (which is perhaps more effective than force), where the command lies with the true sovereign, where the rich buy pleasures and not authority, I do not see the necessity to destroy a citizen, unless his death were a true and unique deterrence to others from committing crimes—the second reason which I believe would be a just and necessary punishment of death.

The experience of all the centuries has shown that the ultimate penalty has never stopped men's determination to injure society. Take the examples of the Roman citizenry;[2] and of the twenty years reign by the empress Elizabeth of Moscow[3] who gave the fathers of all peoples an example amounting to at least as many conquests bought with the blood of the sons of the fatherland. If these examples do not persuade men to whom the language of reason is always suspect and subject to facile authority, it is enough to consult human nature to perceive the truth of my assertion.

It is not the intensity of punishment that has the greatest effect on the human mind, but its duration; for our sensibility is more easily and surely affected by minimal but repeated impressions than by a strong but fleeting one. The universal power of habit dominates every sentient being, and with its help man talks, walks and satisfies his needs. In this way moral thoughts are imprinted on the mind only by lasting and repeated stimuli. It is not the terrible but momentary spectacle of death of the wicked, but the long and labored example of a man deprived of liberty—who, having become the beast of burden, repays with his toil the society he has offended—that is the strongest deterrent against crime. This is a useful mechanism because it is often repeated within us when we say to ourselves: *I will be reduced to a long and miserable condition if I commit similar misdeeds*—a much more powerful thought than that of death, which men always hold at a murky distance.

The punishment of death makes an impression whose force is not enough to overcome man's natural tendency to forget even essential things, often especially accelerated by the passions. A general rule: violent passions astonish men, but not for long, and are therefore ideal for making revolutions that turn ordinary men into Persians or Lacedaemonians;[4] but in a free and tranquil government the impressions of punishment must be more frequent rather than strong.[5]

The punishment of death is a spectacle for most people and for others an object of compassion mixed with disdain: both these sentiments occupy the minds of the spectators instead of the salutary terror that the laws seek to inspire. But in a moderate and lasting punishment such salutary terror is the dominant sentiment because it is the only one. The limits that the legislator should apply to regulate punishment are conditioned by the sentiment of compassion, when it begins to spread to everyone and into the minds of the witnesses to a punishment directed more to them than to the offender.

[For a punishment to be just its intensity should be only that sufficient to deter men from crime. Now, there is no person who, upon reflection, would choose total and lasting loss of his liberty for whatever advantage he gained from his crime: the intensity[6] of punishment of perpetual slavery is enough to thwart any determined mind so it is therefore a substitute for death. Let me add something more: A great many regard death in a calm and cold light, some through fanaticism, some through vanity which almost always accompanies them even beyond their graves, and some in a final and desperate attempt to live no more or to escape misery. But neither fanaticism nor vanity can hold up between fetters and chains, under the rod, under the yoke, or in an iron cage, where the desperate criminal does not end his suffering, but just begins it.[7] Our minds resist violence and extreme but momentary pain more than the pain of time and unrelenting boredom; thus we are able to cope with the fleeting pain of the former and take a breath; but this mental adaptability is not enough to resist the long and repeated stimuli of the latter. The punishment of death sets an example to the nation for one crime; but the punishment of perpetual slavery for one crime gives many and lasting examples. Also, if it is important that men often take note of the power of the laws, the punishments of death must be frequent: but this presupposes that there are frequent crimes to be punished. So for the death penalty to be as useful as it could be, it must not have the total effect on men it should, that is, it should be useful and useless at the same time. To whoever might say that perpetual slavery is as painful as death, and therefore equally cruel, I reply that by adding up all the unhappy moments of slavery would perhaps be more, but these accumulate over an entire lifetime, while the death penalty exerts its force in a single moment. This is the advantage of the punishment of slavery, which frightens those who see it more than those who suffer it, for the former see the total of all the unhappy moments, and the latter suffer the unhappiness of a single moment in the here and now, with no mind to the future. All the evils are magnified in the imagination, and those who suffer it find help and consolation unknown and unacknowledged by the spectators, who substitute their own sensibility for the wretch's hardened soul.]

Here, more or less, is the reasoning of a thief or an assassin, who has no counterweight for not violating the laws except for the gallows or the wheel. I know that to develop a clear understanding of one's state of mind is an art that is obtained only through education; but because a thief may not be able to express his state of mind does not mean that it does not take effect. Why should I respect laws that leave so great a gap between me and the rich man? He denies me the small change that I look to him for, and his excuse is to order me to toil at work of which he knows nothing. Who has made these laws? Rich and powerful men, who never deign to visit the squalid huts of the poor, who have never divided moldy bread among the tears of their wives and the innocent cries of their starving children. We break these bonds that are fatal to the majority and useful only to a few indolent tyrants. We attack injustice at its source. I will return to my natural state of self sufficiency. I will live free and happy for such time on the fruits of my courage and my industry. Perhaps there will come a day of grief and regret, but this time will be brief, and I will have had a day of hardship for many years of liberty and pleasure. King only of a few,[8] I will correct the errors of lady luck, and I will see the tyrants blanch and tremble at the presence of one whom, with insulting pomp, they place below their horses and their dogs.

Then religion confronts the mind of the wicked criminal, who abuses everyone and everything, by offering him an easy repentance and almost certain eternal happiness, thus diminishing much of the horror of the ultimate tragedy. But if he looks ahead a great number of years or over the course of a life that will pass in slavery and the grief suffered in front of his own countrymen with whom now he lives in freedom and friendship, he will see by comparison that he is a slave of the very laws by which he was protected, and he will make a salutary comparison between all this and the uncertain fruits of his crime in the short time he could possibly have enjoyed them. The constant example of those whom he actually sees as victims of their own negligence, has a much greater effect on him than the spectacle of a cruel punishment that hardens more than corrects.

The punishment of death is not useful because of the example of atrocity it gives to men. If the passions or the necessity of war have taught us to shed human blood, the laws moderating our conduct should not add another example so much more horrid when lawful death is administered with such studious formality. In the midst of this absurdity the laws, which are the expression of public will, which proscribe and punish murder, commit one and the same crime, and, to deter citizens from assassination, order a public one. Which laws are true and more useful? Those pacts and conditions that all would observe and propose, while avoiding the ever present voice of private interests or combining them with those of the public. What are the sentiments of everyone on the punishment of death? We read of them in the acts of indignation and depression the contempt with which everyone regards the executioner who is but an innocent executor of the public will, a good citizen who contributes to the public good, the necessary instrument of internal public security, as valued as soldiers are outside. What then is the origin of this contradiction? Because this sentiment is inscribed in the human heart to the shame of reason? Because men, in the utmost secrecy of their minds, want more than anything else to preserve the original form of their ancient state of nature, having always believed that one's life can never truly be under the power of others, except of necessity, that, with its iron scepter, rules the universe.

What must men think when they see wise judges and grave priests of justice who, with indifferent tranquility and mechanical slowness drag a criminal to his death, and during his miserable spasms of final agony as he awaits the fatal blow, a judge with unfeeling coldness, perhaps also with secret satisfaction of his own authority, goes to enjoy the comforts and pleasures of life? *Ah! They will say, these laws are but a pretext for force and reflect the premeditated and cruel formality of justice; they are but a language of conventions to immolate us with greater security, as victims destined to be sacrificed to the insatiable idol of despotism. Assassination is presented to us as a terrible misdeed, yet it is accepted without repugnance or fury. Let us profit from this example. Looking upon a violent death is a terrible scene as it is described to us, but we see it as a momentary event. How much less terrible it will be for someone who, because he is not expecting it, is saved from almost all the pain there is in it?*[9] Such are the false and contorted arguments that, if not clearly, at least in confusion, are made by those men disposed to crime, in whom as we have seen, the abuse of religion is more powerful than religion itself.

If I am countered by the example that almost all centuries and all nations have the death penalty for some crimes, I reply that it flies in the face of truth against which there is no prescription, that the history of men gives the idea of an immense sea of errors, in which few and confused truths float at great distance one from another. Human sacrifices have been common in almost all nations, and who would excuse them? That some small society has only for a short time abstained from administering the death penalty, favors me rather than the contrary position because it falls in the lot of all great truths, whose duration is as a flash of lightning compared to the long and dark night which envelops mankind. The fortunate epoch in which truth exceeds error has not yet arrived, and only those truths that infinite Wisdom has chosen to separate by revealing them have been exempted from this universal law.[10] The voice of one philosopher is too weak against the tumult and shouting of so many who are blinded by custom, but a few sages who are scattered over the face of the earth will in their heart of hearts echo what I say. And if truth could overcome, among the infinite obstacles keeping it from a monarch and in spite of him, reach his throne, let him know that it will arrive there with the secret affirmation of all mankind; let him know that it will keep silent in his presence the bloody fame of conquerors and that a just posterity will assign him first place among the peaceful trophies of the Tituses, of the Antonines and the Trajans.[11]

What a happy circumstance if, for the first time, the laws should be made for humanity, now that we see beneficent monarchs on the thrones of Europe, inspiring peaceful virtues, the sciences, the arts, serving as crowned citizens and fathers of the people. This is the kind of authority that makes for happy subjects because it keeps at bay an intermediate despotism[12] (more cruel because less secure), which suffocates the always sincere will of the people, a will much more auspicious when directly linked to the throne! I say, if these monarchs allow these ancient laws to continue, it is because of the infinite difficulty of removing from these errors the venerated rust of many centuries. For this reason enlightened citizens will desire with greater ardor the continued growth of their own authority.

§ XXIX. Preventive Detention

A common error working against social utility (the true purpose of which is to foster personal security) is to allow the judge, who is in charge of enforcing the law, to interpret the laws for imprisoning a citizen, to take away the liberty of an enemy for frivolous pretexts, or to leave unpunished a friend, despite the strongest evidence of guilt. Preventive detention in prison is a punishment that, quite different from every other punishment, must of necessity precede the finding of guilt. However, this special characteristic does not negate the other essential, which is that only the laws determine the cases in which a man should be punished. Therefore the law should indicate the circumstantial evidence that justifies custody of the accused in order to subject him to interrogation and punishment. Notoriety of the accused, his flight, his extrajudicial confession,[1] the confession of an accomplice, threats and continued hostility against the victim, the facts of the crime (the existence of corpus delicti), and similar clues are sufficient proof to incarcerate a citizen; but these proofs must be assessed by the law not by judges whose decrees are always opposed to political liberty, except possibly when they are particular expressions of a general maxim included in the public code. The laws will be content with weaker evidence to justify incarceration only when punishments are more moderate, when the squalor and hunger of prison are removed, when compassion and humanity penetrate their iron doors and contain the inexorable and obdurate ministers of justice. A man accused of a crime, incarcerated then absolved should not endure any trace of public infamy. How many Romans accused of serious crimes, then found innocent, were revered by the people and honored with public positions! So, for what reason is the destiny of an innocent so different in our times? Because it seems that, in the present criminal justice system according to people's opinion, the ideas of force and power prevail over justice; because they throw both the accused and convicted indiscriminately into the same cavern; because prison is used as a punishment rather than confinement of the accused; [[and because internal force as the hand maiden of the laws is completely separated from that used externally to defend the throne and the nation, in which case the two should be united. In this way, through the common sanction of the laws, the internal use of force is combined with judicial control, but is not dependent on it for its immediate power. And the glory that accompanies the pomp and ceremony of a military corps should eradicate infamy, which is more akin to the way things are done rather than to the thing itself, as are all popular sentiments. This is demonstrated by military prisons which in common opinion are not so shameful as are prisons for criminals]]. Yet in the people, in their customs and laws, which always are more than a century behind in comparison to the contemporary enlightenment of a nation, still surviving are the barbarous impressions and ferocious ideas of our ancestors, who were huntsmen from the North.[2] Some have argued that a crime, that is, an act against the law, should be punished without regard to the place where it was committed, as if the status of being a subject were indelible, the same or even worse than being a slave, as if a man could live in one country and be subjected to the dominion of another, and thus his actions could be without contradiction subordinated to both sovereigns and two often contradictory codes. Others believe similarly that an act of cruelty committed, for example, in Constantinople, may be punished in Paris, for the abstract reason that he who offends humanity deserves all of humanity's hostility and universal condemnation, as though the judged would be the vindicators of the emotions of men rather than of the pacts which bind men together. The place of punishment is the place of the crime[3] because only there and nowhere else are men forced to act against a private person in order to prevent a public offence. A wicked person, but one who has not broken a contract with a society of which he is not a member, may be feared, and therefore by the superior force of society exiled and excluded, but not punished with the formality of the laws that are vindicators of agreements, rather than of the intrinsic evil of actions.

Those guilty of lesser crimes are usually punished, with the obscurity of prison, or sent, to give an example, almost useless because far away, into slavery in nations against whom they had not offended.[4] If men are not induced by a single moment to commit very serious crimes, they will consider public punishment for a grave misdeed as remote and unlikely to happen to them. But the public punishment of less serious crimes which are uppermost in their minds, will make an impression that, while deterring, will deter them from others more distant. Punishment must not only be proportionate to the force of the crimes, but also in the way it is inflicted.[5] Some are freed from punishment for a small crime when the person offended pardons him, an act while of beneficence to all humanity, is against the public good. For although a private citizen may mitigate the crime with his forgiveness, he may not, by example, condone the damage of the offense to society. The right to punish is not of one person, but of all citizens and the sovereign. He may renounce his own portion of right, but this does not annul the right of others.

§ XXX. Criminal Proceedings and the Statute of Limitations[1]

Once the evidence of the crime has been collected and its certainty assessed, it is necessary to allow the offender the time and reasonable opportunity to justify himself, but the time must be brief enough not to interfere with his prompt punishment, which we have seen is one of the main principles of deterring crimes. A misguided love of humanity seems to oppose this limit in time, but any doubt about it will vanish when one reflects on the dangers to innocents that result from defects of legislation.

However the laws must fix a specific period of time for the defense of the offender and collection of evidence, otherwise the judge would become the legislator if he were to decide on the time necessary to prove the crime. Similarly, atrocious crimes, which men remember for a long time, when they are proven, do not merit any statute of limitations in favor of an offender who has escaped punishment by flight. But in minor and hidden crimes there must be a statute of limitations to remove any uncertainty of the citizen's fate, because the obscurity in which the crimes are involved for a long time removes the example of impunity, leaving the possibility for the offender to improve his situation. It is enough for me just to outline these principles, because a precise limit can only be fixed for a given legislation in given circumstances of a society. I add only that, given the proven utility of moderate punishment in a nation, the laws that decrease or increase the time after which the crime is no longer prosecutable or the time of judicial enquiry needed for evidence collection, in proportion to the gravity of crimes—which makes incarceration itself or voluntary exile part of the punishment—will produce an easy classification of a few mild punishments for a great number of crimes.

However these time limits should not increase in exact proportion to the atrocity of crimes because the probability of crimes is the inverse of their atrocity. Thus the time for the judicial enquiry should be decreased and the time allowed for prosecution increased. This would seem to contradict what I said before—that I am assigning equal punishments

81

for unequal crimes by counting as punishment the time incarcerated and the procedural requirements preceding the sentence. To explain more specifically my idea, I distinguish two classes of crimes: the first is that of atrocious crimes, beginning with homicide and including all the other grave offences. The second is that of minor crimes. This distinction has its foundation in human nature. The security of life is a natural right, the security of property is a social right.[2] The motives that drive men beyond their natural sentiment of compassion are far fewer than the motives that, because of the natural desire to be happy, compel them to break a right which they do not find in their hearts, but in conventions of society. The greatest difference in probability of innocence of these two classes is that they are regulated by different principles. In more atrocious crimes, because they are rare, the time for judicial examination must be diminished because of the increased probability that the accused is innocent. But the amount of time for procedural requirements must be increased because a definitive verdict of the innocence or guilt of a man will remove the hope of impunity, which grows with the atrocity of the crime. But in minor crimes the probability of the offender's innocence decreases, so the time for examination must increase and, since the harm of impunity is less, the time taken by procedural requirements must be diminished. Such a distinction between these two classes of crimes should not be allowed, if the harm of impunity were to decrease as the probability of the crime increases. [[It should be considered that an accused, who is neither innocent or guilty, though freed for lack of evidence, may later be prosecuted for the same crime if new evidence emerges as indicated by the laws, resulting in a new incarceration and a new examination, so long as the time fixed for this crime by the statute of limitations has not passed. This at least is the spirit of what seems to me the most efficacious way to defend both the security and liberty of the subjects, while ensuring that one is not favored at the expense of the other. For if it were, these two blessings, which underwrite the inalienable and equal patrimony of every citizen, will not be preserved or protected, one from open or disguised despotism, the other from the turbulence of popular anarchy.]]

§ XXXI. Crimes Difficult to Prove

In view of these principles it may seem strange to one who has never thought about it, that reason has rarely been the legislator of nations; that crimes either the more atrocious or more hidden and chimerical—that is, the least probable—are proven by argument or by weak or equivocal evidence. It is as if the laws and judges have no interest in finding the truth, but only to prove the crime, so much so that the prospect of the offender's innocence is viewed as a danger which exceeds the probability of the actual crime. For the most part men lack the vigor that is equally necessary to commit either grave crimes or to perform acts of great virtue, so the two always seem to occur at the same time in those nations that are supported by a dynamic government and by passions oriented to the public good, rather than by the masses or by the constant goodness of the laws. In these nations the weakened passions seem to be more suited to maintaining rather than improving the form of government. An important conclusion follows from this: that the greatest crimes in a nation do not always constitute a proof of its decadence.

There are some crimes that are frequent in society and at the same time difficult to prove, and in these the difficulty of proof lies in the probability of innocence. Since in these cases the harm deriving from impunity is much less a concern because the frequency of the crimes' occurrence depends on principles different from the danger of impunity, the time allowed both for judicial enquiry and for starting criminal prosecution must diminish equally. Yet adultery and Grecian lust,[1] which are crimes difficult to prove, are those that, according to the principles received promote tyrannical presumptions: the *almost proven,* the *semi-proven* (as though a man could be *semi-innocent* or *semi-guilty,* that is *semi-punishable* and *semi-absolvable.*) This is where torture exercises its cruel tyranny on the person of the accused, in the testimony, and even in the poor wretch's family—in conformity with the teaching of some educated men who, with iniquitous coldness, set up the normative standards for judges.

Adultery is a crime that, considered politically, has its own force and direction for two reasons: the laws of men vary and the very strong attraction that pulls one sex to the other. In many ways this attraction is similar to how gravity moves the universe, particularly that it decreases with distance, and just as the one regulates all the movements of heavenly bodies, the other nearly all those of the human spirit throughout its duration. But they are dissimilar to the extent that gravity achieves a state of equilibrium when obstacles are placed in its way, whereas the other grows with force and vigor.

If I were to speak to nations still deprived of the light of religion I would say that there is still another serious difference between adultery and other crimes. It is born of abuse of an unending need that is universal to all humanity, a primary need, the foundation of society itself, whereas other destructive crimes have their origin determined by the passions of the moment rather than from a natural need. This need appears to one who knows the history of man, to be a monotonous condition occurring in the same climate in constant quantity.[2] If this were true, laws and customs aimed to reduce the sum total would be useless, or, worse, pernicious because their effect would be to burden some with the needs of others, in addition to their own. But on the contrary, those laws would be wise, which, following the easy inclination of the plain, so to speak, would separate and diffuse the sum into many equal and smaller quantities, which would uniformly prevent both aridity or inundation in all places.

Conjugal fidelity is always proportioned to the number and freedom of marriages. Where hereditary prejudices govern them, where domestic power[3] arranges and dissolves them, there gallantry,[4] in spite of vulgar morality, breaks their ties in secret, officially declaring itself against the effects, while pardoning its causes. But there is no need for such reflections for those who, living in true religion, have more sublime motives which correct the force of these natural effects. The action of one such crime is so instantaneous and mysterious, so hidden by the veil placed over it by the laws—a necessary but fragile veil that adds esteem instead of reducing it. The occasions for it are so easy, the consequences so doubtful, that it is more in the hand of the legislator to prevent it than to correct it. A general rule: for every crime that, by its nature, must on most occasions remain unpunished, the punishment becomes an incentive. It is a property of our imagination that a difficulty, if not insurmountable or too difficult for the lazy mind of every man, excites a more lively imagination and grandiose idea of the object. The difficulties are such that when many barriers impede the wandering and voluble imagination which desires the object, and constrain it from overwhelming all relationships, the more it attaches itself closely to pleasure, to which our mind is naturally inclined, rather than to pain and suffering, from which it flees away as far as it can.

The crime of pederasty is so severely punished by the laws and so easily subjected to the torments that dominate innocence, that it derives less from the needs of man isolated and free than from the passions of a man in society and a slave. It gets its force not so much from the satisfaction of pleasure, but from the education which begins to render all men useless to themselves but at the same time to make them useful to others. This is the effect produced by those institutions[5] where the vigor of youth is concentrated, where, blocked by an insurmountable barrier from all commerce,[6] all the vigor of nature is wasted and becomes useless for humanity, as it accelerates the coming of old age.

Infanticide[7] is equally the result of an inevitable dilemma in which a woman is placed, when she is seduced through weakness or violence. If she must choose between her shame and the suppression of a being not yet conscious of death as evil, how could she not prefer the latter to the certain misery she and her unhappy offspring would suffer? A better way to prevent this crime would be to protect with useful laws the weak against tyranny, which exaggerates vices that cannot be hidden by the mantle of virtue.

I do not pretend to diminish the justifiable outrage deserved by these crimes, but, by uncovering their origins, I believe it is right to extract the general conclusion, which is that a punishment of a crime cannot be called precisely just (that is to say, necessary) so long as the law has not adopted the best means possible in the given circumstances of a nation, to prevent it.

§ XXXII. Suicide

Strictly speaking, suicide is a crime that does not seem amenable to punishment because it can only be applied to innocent persons or on a cold and insensible body. If the latter, then punishment makes no more impression on the living than the whipping of a statue. If the former, it is unjust and tyrannical, because the political liberty of men requires that even if suicide were a crime, innocent family members should not be punished. Men love life so much, and all that surrounds them confirms them in this love. The seductive images of pleasure and hope, the most delicious deceiver of mortals, for which they swallow a huge mouthful of evil mixed with a few drops of contentment, entices men just too much. Thus one need not fear that the unavoidable impunity of this crime will have any influence over men. Whoever fears pain obeys the laws, but death extinguishes in the body all sources of pain. What then will be the motive to restrain the desperate hand of the suicide?

Whoever kills himself commits a lesser evil against society than one who steps out of society's constraints completely, because the former leaves all his possessions behind, but the latter, at least in part, keeps them with him. Furthermore, if the power of society consists in the number of its citizens, then to subtract one of them and give him to a neighboring nation causes a double injury compared to the suicide who simply by his death removes himself from society. So this question is reduced to knowing whether it is useful or damaging to a nation to allow any of its members to migrate elsewhere.

All laws that are not sustained by force or, due to the nature of circumstances, are rendered ineffective, should not be promulgated. And as opinion dominates the minds of men, so it obeys the slow and indirect impressions of the legislator and resists those that are direct and violent. Thus the many useless laws that are despised by men, communicate to them belittlement of the laws even those that are more beneficial. They are regarded as more of an obstacle to overcome rather than as the depositary of the public good. So if, as already said, our sentiments are limited, to the extent that men have veneration for objects outside the law, they will have less for those same laws. From this principle the wise dispenser of public happiness may draw some useful conclusions, which, were I to expound on them, would take me too far from my subject. And my subject is to prove the uselessness in making the state a prison. Such a law is useless because, except where impassable cliffs or non-navigable seas separate a country from all others, how can one close all points of its circumference? And who will guard the guards?[1] One who carries all his possessions away from his country cannot be punished for having done so. Besides, once this crime has been committed it cannot be punished any more, and to punish it before it was committed would be to punish men's intent and not their actions. It is an attempt to control intent, the most important part of man's freedom from the imperiousness of human laws. [[To direct punishment against the goods and chattel than an expatriate has left behind—putting aside the inevitable collusion that could not be prevented from corrupting contracts— would bring to a standstill all commerce between nations.]] To punish the offender upon his return would impede rather than repair the damage done to society because it would cause all expatriates to stay away permanently. To prohibit a person from leaving his country adds to the desire of nationals to leave and is a warning to foreigners to stay out.[2]

What must we think of a government that has no other way than fear to retain its citizens who are naturally attached to their country through the first impressions of childhood? The sure way to attach citizens to their country is to add to the relative good of everyone. Just as we must make sure that the balance of trade is in our favor, so it is in the greatest interest of the sovereign and of the nation that the sum of happiness compared to that of surrounding nations, is also in our favor. The pleasures of luxury are not the principle elements of this happiness, though they are a necessary remedy of inequality, which grows as nations develop, without which remedy wealth could become concentrated in the grip of a single person.[3] Where the boundaries of a nation expand at a greater rate than its population there luxury favors the despot, [[because the fewer men there are the less small industry there is; and the less small industry the greater the dependence of the poor on lavish handouts, so there is greater difficulty for the oppressed to unite against the oppressors and less to fear as well. The adoration, ceremonial offices, distinctions and tributes that create a greater sense of distance between the powerful and the weak]] are more easily attained by the few rather than the many. For men are more independent when under less scrutiny, and under less scrutiny when they are more numerous.[4] But where the population grows at a greater rate than its country's borders, luxury is at odds with despotism because of the spirit of industry and the activity of men. The needs of the poor also provide so many pleasures and comforts to the rich people, thus contrasting their attitude of ostentation, which fosters sentiments of dependence.

Therefore it is possible to observe that in vast states that are weak and depopulated, putting aside other obstacles or reasons, ostentatious luxury prevails over that of convenience; but in states with larger populations the luxury of convenience always diminishes that of ostentation.[5] But traffic and trade in luxury has this inconvenience, that however many may participate in it, luxury begins with a few, and ends with a few, and only a very tiny part is tasted by the majority, such that it does not impede the feeling of misery that hinges more on relative comparison than on reality. But personal security and liberty are limited only by the laws that form the basic principles of happiness, and by these pleasures of luxury favor the population, without which they would become the instrument of tyranny. Whereas the most noble of beasts and the freest of birds retreat far away in solitude and inaccessible woods, and they abandon the fertile and joyous fields to the trapper, so men likewise flee those same pleasures when offered by tyranny.[6]

It is thus demonstrated that the law that imprisons subjects in their own country[7] is useless and unjust. So the same should apply to the punishment of suicides, and therefore—not withstanding the fault that God can punish because only He can punish after death—suicide is not a crime of any business to men since the punishment, instead of hurting the offender, hurts only his family. If someone objects that such a punishment can nevertheless restrain a man determined to kill himself, I respond: one who renounces all the good in life, who hates his existence here and would prefer eternal unhappiness, is hardly likely to be restrained by the less effective and distant punishment of his children and relatives.

§ XXXIII. Smuggling

Smuggling is a crime that truly offends the sovereign and the nation, but in this case the punishment should not shame the offender because its commission is not denounced by public opinion. Thus, to give shameful punishment for a crime that does not affect the reputations of men only reduces the feeling of shame of those who do it. For example to give the same punishment of death to one who kills a wild pheasant and one who assassinates a man or falsifies an important document, makes no discrimination between these crimes. This undermines the moral sentiments of man—the work of many centuries and of much bloodshed, slowly and with difficulty produced in the human mind, born with the help of such sublime motives and an extensive edifice of strict formality.[1]

This crime is born of the law itself, for the higher the import taxes, the greater advantage to the offender. Therefore the temptation to smuggling and ease of doing it increase according to length of borders and merchandise available that is small in bulk.[2] The punishment of confiscating either the stolen goods or things that go with them is certainly just, but would be much more useful if there were a lower tax, because men will take risks only in proportion to the advantage they can get from the expected reward produced by the undertaking.[3]

But why does this crime never cause shame in its author, since it is a theft against the sovereign, and consequently the nation itself? I respond that offenses which men believe cannot be committed against them do not interest them enough to produce public indignation against those who commit them. This is the case with smuggling. Men on whom remote consequences make a weak impression do not see the damage that could affect them from smuggling, and in fact they enjoy its present advantages. Nor do they see the damage done to the sovereign. They are then less interested in denigrating the smuggler compared to those who commit a private theft, forgery, and other evils that they themselves may suffer. The principle is clear that every sensitive person is interested only in those evils that he knows about.

But should such a crime go unpunished against one who has neither money nor property to lose? No: there are some types of smuggling that affect public revenue (so essential and such a difficult aspect of good legislation), that such a crime deserves a considerable punishment even prison or servitude—but prison and servitude that match the nature of the crime itself. For example, prison for smuggling tobacco should not be the same as for assassin or thief. So limiting the smuggler's labors to work and service to the royal treasury that he wished to defraud, would be a better fit to the nature of the crime.[4]

§ XXXIV. Debtors

The good faith of contracts and the security of commerce constrain the legislator to secure for creditors the persons of bankrupt debtors, but I believe it important to distinguish between the fraudulent bankrupt and the innocent bankrupt.[1] The former must be punished with the same punishment that is assigned to counterfeiters, because to falsify the weight of metal in coins, which represents a pledge to the obligations of all citizens, is no more serious a crime than falsifying the obligation itself. [[But what of the innocent bankrupt, who, after a rigorous examination has proved to his judges that by some other fraud, disgrace or event unavoidable by human prudence, he has been stripped of his possessions, for what barbarous motive must he be thrown in prison? Sadly he is deprived of the only good thing he has left, simple liberty, to suffer the distress of guilt, and the desperation of his impugned integrity. He may even doubt his own innocence which he had enjoyed in a tranquil life under the tutelage of the laws which he could in no way avoid offending—laws dictated by the powerful for the greedy, and suffered by the weak for the sake of hope that glimmers in the human spirit. So how can we believe that only bad things happen to others and the good things happen to ourselves? Men, left to their own devices, love cruel laws however much they are subject to those same laws, even though it should be in their interest to foster moderation, because the fear of being offended against is greater than the wish to offend. Returning to the innocent bankrupt, I say that though his obligation to pay the full amount cannot be cancelled, though he cannot be granted any exception without the consent of the parties of interest, and although he may take his financial interests to another jurisdiction, he must be bound under threat of punishment to repay in progressive payments the amount in proportion to his earnings. What is the legitimate pretext, as in safe commerce, as in the sacred ownership of property, that justifies the privation of liberty, useless to his creditors, unless putting the supposed innocent bankrupt through the evils of slavery reveals his secrets,[2] a very rare possibility after a rigorous inquiry? I believe the legislative maxim that the value of political inconveniencies varies in direct proportion to the damage to the public and in inverse proportion to the improbability of verifying it.[3] One should be able to distinguish fraud from grave fault, serious from less serious, and perfect innocence from all; and by assigning to the first punishments for crimes of forgery, to the second minor punishments such as deprivation of liberty, reserving for the last the free choice by means of restitution, or in the third case take away the free choice and leave it up to his creditors. But the distinctions between serious and less serious must be fixed by blind and impartial laws, not by the dangerous and arbitrary prudence of judges. The fixing of limits is as necessary in politics as in mathematics, no less in assessing the public good as in measuring dimension itself.[*]

How easily might a provident legislator impede a large part of fraudulent bankruptcies and repair the disgrace of innocent and industrious individuals! The public and open registration of all contracts, and the freedom of all citizens to consult the documents in a well organized way, a public bank founded on wisely selected taxes on thriving trade and designed to assist its unfortunate and blameless members: this would cause no real inconvenience and produce innumerable advantages. But the easiest, the simplest and the best laws do not wait for the sign of approval of the legislator to expand abundance and strength in the bosom of the nation, laws that would receive the everlasting praise and thanks of generation after generation; such laws are either the less known or wanted. A restless and shallow spirit, timid prudence of the present moment, and an obsessive wariness of new things take possession of the sentiments of those who make up the throng of actions of small mortals.]]

---

[a]   *Author's note* [[Commerce and private property are not a goal of the social contract, but they can be a means to obtaining it. To expose all the members of society to the evils of which there are so many combinations would result in subordinating the end to the means, an invalid argument in the sciences, especially in politics, into which I fell in preceding editions*. There I said that the innocent bankrupt must be placed in custody as a pledge for his debts, or to work them off as a slave for his creditors. I am ashamed to have written this. I have been accused of sacrilege and I did not deserve it. I have been accused of sedition, and I did not deserve it. I have offended the rights of humanity, and no one has reprimanded me for it**.]]

**   Up to the fourth edition of the *Treatise*.

§ XXXV. Sanctuaries

I return now to examine two questions: One, whether sanctuaries are just,[1] and whether the agreement between nations[2] for the exchange of offenders is useful or not. There must be no place inside the borders of a country that is independent of the laws. They must be able to follow every citizen, just as the shadow follows the body. Impunity and sanctuary do not differ much, and the impression of the punishment consists more in its certainty rather than its severity. Sanctuaries invite crimes rather than deter them. To expand sanctuaries is to create a great many little sovereignties, because where laws do not prevail, new laws can conflict with common laws, therefore engendering a spirit that opposes the very core of society. All of history tells us that great revolutions in states and in the opinions of men grow out of sanctuaries. But whether the exchange of offenders between nations is useful, I would not dare to decide this question until the laws conform more closely with the needs of humanity, the punishments more mild, and dependence on arbitrariness and opinion are ended; until the laws provide sanctuary for innocence oppressed and virtue detested; until tyranny is confined to the vast lands of Asia by universal reason, which always unites the interests of the throne with its subjects. Albeit the belief that one cannot find a patch of ground where crimes are condoned would be the most efficacious means of preventing them.[3]

§ XXXVI. Bounties

Another question is whether it is useful to place a price on the head of a man known to be guilty, by arming every citizen and so making each one into an executioner. Either the offender is outside the country's borders or inside: in the former the sovereign encourages citizens to commit a crime and exposes them to punishment, which causes injury and usurpation of his authority over other men. By these actions he authorizes other nations to do the same to himself. The latter case reveals the sovereign's true weakness. He who has the power to defend himself does not seek to buy it. Even more, such a decree upsets all moral ideas and virtue, which at the slightest breeze may vanish from the human mind. Now the laws invite treachery and now they punish it. With one hand the legislator strengthens the bonds of the family, relatives and friends, and with the other rewards those who attack and break them. Always contradicting himself, now the legislator welcomes the suspicious minds of men into his confidence, now he sows distrust in all their hearts. Instead of preventing a crime, he inspires a hundred. These are the expediencies of weak nations, whose laws are but the quick repairs of a ruined edifice that crumbles in every respect. To the extent that a nation grows more enlightened, good faith and reciprocal trust become necessary and these are most often identified with good politics. The artifices, the cabals, the obscure and devious ways, are thus more often anticipated, and the sentiment of all drives back the sentiment of each particular individual.[1] Those centuries of ignorance, in which public morality cowed men to obey private interests, offer illuminating lessons and experience for the enlightened epochs. But the laws that reward treachery and excite clandestine wars, spreading mutual suspicion among citizens, oppose this very necessary reunion of morals and politics, to which men owe their happiness, nations their peace, and the universe a longer interval of tranquility and rest from evils that go on around us.

§ XXXVII. [Attempts, Accomplices, Pardons

Laws do not punish intent. However, a crime that begins with some action that manifests a willingness[1] to follow the action through deserves punishment, but less than the actual execution of that crime. The importance of preventing an attempt justifies the punishment, especially as the interval between the attempt and the execution gives an opportunity for repentance when a greater punishment is reserved for the completed crime. The same applies, but for a different reason, when there are more accomplices to the crime and not all of them were immediately involved in executing it. When more men join together in a risky undertaking, the greater the risk, the more they will try to distribute it equally among themselves. Then it will be more difficult for them to find one who is agreeable to be the executor of the crime, taking on a risk greater than the other accomplices. The only exception would be in the case where an executor had been decided upon beforehand; so in order to equalize the risk, he would have to receive extra compensation for taking on the risk of greater punishment. In this case the punishment established for him and his accomplices should be the same.[2] These reflections may seem too theoretical to one who might not reflect on the greatest utility of laws that, where possible, interfere with the means of accomplices of a crime to agree among themselves.

Some courts offer a pardon to an accomplice of a serious crime who exposes his companions. Such an expedient has disadvantages and advantages. The disadvantages are that the nation authorizes betrayal (perennially detestable among the wicked), and that crimes of courage are less fatal to the nation than those of cowardice because they occur infrequently and simply await a beneficent force and direction to turn them to the public good. Moreover, cowardice is more common and contagious, and always more selfishly motivated. Finally, the court demonstrates the real uncertainty and considerable weakness of the law, if it must beg for help from an offender. The advantages are that it prevents important crimes by revealing their effects and the hidden authors who intimidate the people. As well, it contributes to a view that one who lacks respect for the laws, and therefore the public, will probably be disrespectful in his private life. It seems to me that a general law that promises a pardon to known accomplices of any crime would be preferable to a special declaration in a particular case, because the mutual fear that every accomplice should have of being alone in bearing the risk, should prevent their union. Thus the court should not encourage audacious criminals by requesting their assistance in a particular case. A law such as this, however, should accompany a pardon with banishment of the informer. But I torment myself struggling to overcome the remorse I feel in authorizing betrayal and deception as part of sacrosanct laws, the monument of public trust, the core of human morals. What an example to the nation it would be then, if the law failed to deliver the promised pardon, if by means of learned nitpicking one who had accepted the invitation to the laws were dragged to punishment to the shame of the public trust! These examples are not uncommon among nations, and therefore are certainly not uncommon in those that have no other idea of a nation except that of complicated machinery, the mechanisms of which the more skillful and more powerful operate according to their talents. Cold and insensible to all that forms the delight of tender and sublime minds, with imperturbable wisdom they excite the sentiments more sweet and the passions more violent, whenever they consider it useful to their ends, playing the minds of men as musical instruments.[3]

§ XXXVIII. Suggestive Interrogations, Depositions

Our laws proscribe interrogations that are called *suggestive* in a trial: that is, according to scholars, those which investigate the *specific* in respect to the circumstances of the crime rather than the *general*. Those questions, that is, which have such an immediate connection to the crime that they *suggest* to the offender an immediate response. Interrogations according to criminologists must skirt around the fact, but not take a direct line to it. The reasons for this method are either not to *suggest* to the offender a response that will shield him from the accusation, or perhaps because it seems against the very nature of an offender to accuse himself. No matter for which of these two reasons, it is remarkable that, intrinsic to this practice, the law contradicts itself by authorizing torture. What interrogation could be more *suggestive* than pain? The first reason is verified through torture because pain will *suggest* to a robust accused an obstinate silence so he can exchange a greater punishment for a lesser punishment, and to the weak it will *suggest* a confession to free himself more easily from the torment of the present compared to the pain to come. The same evidence applies to the second reason, because if a *special* interrogation makes an accused confess against his natural right, the spasms of torture will make him do it much more easily. But men regulate themselves more according to the differences in names of things rather than to things themselves. Among other abuses of grammar which have not a little influence on the affairs of men, is when the deposition of an accused who is already condemned and rendered void and useless: a *civil death*, gravely announce the peripatetic legal consultants, and a *dead man* has no capacity for other actions. To sustain this vain metaphor many victims have been sacrificed, and it is often well disputed with the grave reflection that the truth must be sacrificed to juridical formulas. As long as depositions of a condemned offender do not arrive at a point where they obstruct the course of justice, why not make room in the interests of truth—even after the conviction and the extreme misery of the accused—the consideration of new evidence concerning the nature of the crime which may justify a new trial. Formality and ritual are necessary in the administration of justice because nothing should be left to the arbitrariness of the administrator, all of which promotes the idea to the people of a trial neither exciting nor interesting, but stable and regular, because men are imitators and slaves of habit and more easily impressed by sensations than by reasoning. These formalities and rituals must never be fixed by laws in a way that can harm the truth, which, either to be too simple or too complex, needs some external pomp in order to convince the ignorant people.[1] Finally, one who is interrogated and refuses to respond to questioning deserves a punishment fixed by law, and a punishment of the severest kind,[2] so that men may not avoid the necessary example that they owe to the public. This punishment is not necessary when it is beyond doubt that the accused has committed the offence; such interrogations are useless in the same way that the confession of the crime is useless when other proofs already support the conclusion of guilt. This last case is more usual because experience tells us that in the majority of trials the accused pleads not guilty.]

§ XXXIX. On a Particular Kind of Crime

Whoever reads this essay will realize that I have omitted a kind of crime that has covered Europe in human blood and that has built those dreadful piles of living human corpses served as food for the flames, when it was a playful spectacle and pleasing harmony for the blind multitude to hear the pathetic and confused moans of misery that arose from the plumes of black smoke, the smoke of human body parts, with the crackling of charred bones and frying of viscera still quivering.[1] But reasonable men would see that the place, the century and the circumstances do not permit me to examine the nature of this kind of crime.[2] It would take too long and would take me outside my subject to prove how necessary it must be in a state to have a perfect uniformity of thought, contrary to the example of many nations; how opinions, distinguished only by the most subtle and obscure differences that are way beyond the capacity of humans, nevertheless are able to subvert the public good when one of them is authorized in preference for another; and how the nature of opinions is so composed that while some show themselves clearly by mutual fermentation and conflict, the true ones rising to the surface, the false sinking to oblivion, and others, lacking in certainty, having to dress themselves up in authority and power. It would take me too long to prove that, however hateful the commander of force over human minds seems to be, of which the sole achievements are dissimulation followed by humiliation; and however it seems against the spirit of meekness and fraternity which is commanded by reason and by authority that we venerate more, it is nevertheless necessary and indispensable. All of this must be taken as demonstrably proven and in conformity with the true interests of men, provided that it is expounded by one who is an acknowledged authority. I speak only of crimes that emanate from human nature or the social contract, and not of sins[3] of which even temporal punishments must be regulated through other principles than those of a limited philosophy.

§ XL. False Ideas of Utility

A fountain of errors and injustices are the false ideas of utility that are formed by legislators. The false idea of utility is that which places particular inconveniences before general inconveniences, that which controls the sentiments instead of exciting them, that commands logic: submit! A false idea of utility is one that sacrifices a thousand real advantages for an inconvenience either imaginary or of little consequence, that would take fire from men because it burns or water because of the risk of drowning, that cannot repair evils other than by destroying them.[1] [[Laws that prohibit the carrying of arms are laws of that nature. They disarm only those who are not inclined or determined to commit crimes. And all the while, those who have the courage to violate the most sacred laws and the most important of the codes, how will they respect even the minor or purely arbitrary laws? These they can break more easily and with impunity, and which, precisely obeyed, are those laws that would take away personal liberty—so dear to man, so dear to the enlightened legislator—and would subject the innocent to all the vexations that should be those of the accused. These laws worsen the plight of the assaulted, but improve those of the assailants. They do not lessen homicides, but increase them, because the confidence of carrying out an assault against the disarmed is greater than against the armed.[2] These laws are not preventive ones, but born out of the fear of crime. They are born of the tumultuous impression of some particular facts, not from reasoned consideration of the inconveniences and advantages of universal decrees.]] A false idea of utility is that which would impose on a multitude of sensible beings a symmetry and order that makes them brutish and lifeless.[3] It ignores the present that alone affects the multitude through continuity and strength, instead giving strength to distant things, which make only a brief and weak impression unless it is an imagined force, not natural in humanity, and unable to make up for its increased remoteness from the object.[4] Finally, a false idea of utility is that which, sacrificing a thing to a name, splits the public good from the good of all individuals. There is a difference between the state of society and the state of nature. Primitive man damages others only enough to satisfy his needs, but civilized man is sometimes moved by bad laws to offend against others without doing any good for himself. Despotic man sows fear and destruction in the mind of its slaves, but they rebound and return with greater force to torment him. The more solitary and domestic is fear the less dangerous it is to one who makes it the means to his own happiness.[5] But the more public it is and the greater the multitude that is agitated, the easier it is for one, either imprudent, desperate or audacious, to make others serve his own ends, inspiring in them grateful sentiments that are all the more seductive because the risk of the enterprise falls mostly on others. Besides, the value that the unhappy put on the damage to their own existence diminishes in proportion to the misery that they suffer. This is the reason why offenses spawn new offenses, that hatred is a sentiment more lasting than love, why the former gains in strength from repeated acts at the expense of the weakness of the latter.[6]

§ XLI. How to Prevent Crimes

It is better to prevent crimes than to punish them.[1] This is the principal end of all good legislation, which is the art of bringing to men to the greatest happiness, or as they say, the least unhappiness possible according to the calculations of all the good things and all the bad things in life. But so far the means taken to the end are false and in fact opposed to the stated end.[2] It is not possible to reduce the turbulent activity of men to a geometric order without exception and confusion. As constant and very simple laws of nature do not impede the planets disturbing each other in their movements, so in the infinite and totally opposite attractions of pleasure and pain humane laws do not impede turbulence and disorder. Nevertheless this is the chimera of narrow-minded men when they have command in their grip. To prohibit a multitude of indifferent actions does not prevent crimes from occurring, but is instead to create new ones. It is to define virtue and vice by whim rather than as eternal and immutable the way we have been taught. To what will we be reduced if we should be forbidden to do anything that could lead to a crime? It would be necessary to deprive man of the use of his senses. For one motive that pushes men to commit a real crime, there will be a thousand that pushes him to perform those indifferent acts which are called crimes by bad laws. And if the probability of crimes is proportionate to the number of motives, to amplify the sphere of crimes is to increase the probability of committing them. The majority of laws are nothing but privileges, a gift of all to the comfort of a few.[3]

Do you want to prevent crimes? Make sure that the laws are clear, simple, that the strength of the nation is focused on defending them, and no single part of it is employed to destroy them. [Makes sure that the laws favor less the classes of men rather than all men.] Make sure that men fear them, and them only. Fear of laws is beneficial, but men's fear of each other is fatal and productive of crimes. Men who are slaves are more voluptuous, more debauched, more cruel than free men. Free men reflect on the sciences, consider the interests of the nation, take note of great examples and imitate them. But enslaved men, happy with the present day, search amidst the clamor of depravity for a distraction from their hopeless condition. Accustomed to uncertainty in the existence of every thing, and the existence of crimes, to them determined by passions, becomes problematic.[4] If uncertainty of the laws befalls a nation, lazy because of its climate, it maintains and increases that nation's indolence and stupidity. If uncertainty of laws descends on a voluptuous but energetic nation, its energy is dispersed into an infinite number of cabals and intrigues, which sows apathy in every heart and results in treachery and distrust forming the base of prudence. If uncertainty of laws befalls a courageous and strong nation, the uncertainty defeats its purpose, forming at first many oscillations from liberty to slavery, and from slavery back to liberty.

§ XLII. On the Sciences[1]

Do you want to prevent crimes? Make sure that enlightenment accompanies liberty. The evils which knowledge spawns decrease as the diffusion of knowledge increases, and the benefits of this are direct. A bold impostor, who is never an ordinary man, receives the adoration of an ignorant people and the hisses of the enlightened. Knowledge, by facilitating comparisons and a multiplicity of points of view, opposes many sentiments against each other, which are thus reciprocally modified; a process made much easier when they comprehend in others their views and defensiveness the same as in their own. Confronted by the widespread enlightenment of a nation, ignorant calumny and dithering authority are disarmed by reason. However, the vigorous force of the law remains unshaken, because there is no enlightened man who does not love the public, clear and useful contracts of common security, compared to the small portion of his liberty (useless on its own) that he has given up for the highest liberty of all, the liberty of others, without which the laws would conspire against him. Whoever has a sensitive mind, casting a glance over a well constructed legal code, and finding that he has only the liberty to hurt others, will be obliged to bless the throne and he who occupies it.

It is not true that the sciences have always damaged mankind, and if they have it was due to the inevitable evil of men.[2] The multiplication of human kind on the face of the earth introduced war, the cruder arts, the first laws, that were momentary pacts born of necessity and perishing with it. This was the first philosophy of men, containing few elements of justice, because their apathy and lack of wisdom saved them from error.[3] But their needs multiplied more as men multiplied. Then stronger and more lasting impressions were necessary, which deterred them from repeatedly returning to a primitive state of unsociability, making them ever more distressed. Those primitive errors, then, performed a great benefit to all mankind (I mean a great political benefit), because they filled the land with false divinities and created an invisible universe to govern us. The benefactors were those who dared to overtake others and dragged the docile ignorant to the altars. By offering them things that lay beyond their senses, things that flew before them just as they believed they had reached them, but things never scorned because they were never well understood, these benefactors combined and intensified men's conflicted passions into one single object that took over their lives completely. These constituted the first achievements of all nations as they emerged from savagery. It was the epoch when great societies arose, bonded by necessity in this perhaps unique way. I do not speak here of a people chosen by God, for whom most extraordinary miracles and holy visions held human society in place. But as error spreads by perpetually dividing itself, so the sciences that are born of error will make of men a fanatical blind multitude that is buffeted and muddled within a closed labyrinth; not unlike some sensible minds and philosophers who regret the loss of the ancient primal state of the savage. Behold the first epoch, in which consciousness, or more correctly, opinions, are injurious to mankind.

The second epoch represents the difficult and terrible passage from error to truth, from unknown darkness to enlightenment. The immense wielding of errors useful to a few powerful people against truths useful to many of the weak, sought out and fermented the passions which at this time awakened, causing infinite evils and human misery. Whoever reflects on the history of nations (whose principle epochs display similarities after a certain period of time) will find more than once a whole generation sacrificed to the happiness of those who succeed them; but it is a necessary passage from the darkness of ignorance to the light of philosophy, and as a result, from tyranny to liberty. But, when minds have been calmed and the fires that purged nations from their oppressive evils have been extinguished, when truth, which progresses at first slowly and then more rapidly, sits together with the thrones of monarchs and is venerated at the altar of republican parliaments, who could ever maintain that the light that illuminates the multitude is more damaging than darkness, and that understanding the true and simple relationships of things is harmful to mankind?

If blind ignorance is less fatal than partial and confused knowledge, then the evils of he former add to those of the inevitable errors from one who has a restricted vision of what constitutes the truth, then an enlightened man is a very precious gift that a sovereign gives to its nation and to itself, making him the depositary and custodian of sacred laws. Such a man is accustomed to seeing the truth and not fearing it, mostly without the need of others' opinions, which can never be sufficiently satisfied and test the virtue of most men. He becomes used to contemplating humanity from higher points of view, and before his eyes a true nation becomes a family of brothers where the gap between the mighty and the rest of the people seems to him less even as the mass of humanity grows larger. Philosophers acquire needs and interests that are not understood by the common people. Chiefly this means that they do not deny in the public light the principles they have preached in private, and they acquire the habit of loving truth for its own sake. The election of such men forms the happiness of a nation, but only a momentary happiness if good laws are not introduced in such number that they reduce the probability, always great, of a bad decision.

§ XLIII. Judges

Another means to prevent crimes is to interest the executive magistracy in observance of the laws rather than their corruption. The greater the number of judges the less dangerous is the usurpation of the laws, because venality is more difficult among members who watch each other. Their interests in asserting their own authority decrease as the portion of it they can have becomes smaller[1], especially when compared with the danger of the enterprise. If a sovereign with his trappings and pomp, with austerity of edicts, permits just or unjust complaints of one who believes himself oppressed, he will accustom his subjects to fear the magistrates more than the laws. Thus the magistrates will profit more from this fear at the expense of private and public security.

§ XLIV. Rewards[1]

Another way of preventing crimes is that of rewarding virtue. A universal silence of laws of all nations of the day has met this proposal. If the prizes awarded by academies to the discoverers of useful truths have increased our knowledge and good books, why should not prizes distributed by the good hand of the sovereign multiply other virtuous actions?[2] The currency of honor is always inexhaustible and fruitful in the hands of a wise distributor.

§ XLV. Education

Finally the most certain but more difficult means of preventing crime is to improve education, a topic too vast that would take me beyond the bounds of my present project. Still, I dare to speak of this topic because it is a barren field, too close to the intrinsic nature of government to be cultivated by only a few sage men in anticipation of the more remote centuries of public happiness. A great man who enlightens the humanity that persecutes him,[1] sees in the details what are the major principles of true education that are useful to men. This should consist less of a sterile body of facts than the precise selection and analysis of them; it should substitute originals for copies[2] of both moral and physical phenomena as either circumstance or resourcefulness present to the innocent minds of youth; it should guide youth to virtue by the easy path of sentiment and turn it away from evil through the absolute necessity of inconvenience, and not through ambivalent discipline which produces only feigned and momentary obedience.

§ XLVI. [[On Pardons

A measure that punishments are becoming milder is that clemency and pardons become less necessary. Happy would be the nation in which they were considered harmful! Clemency then, this virtue that was at times a substitute for all the duties of the throne, should be excluded in a perfect legislation where the punishment would be milder and the procedure of adjudication regulated and expeditious. This will come as a hard truth to one who lives in the disorder of a criminal justice system where pardon and reprieve are necessary in proportion to the absurdity of the laws and the atrocity of the sentences. In this case it is one of the better prerogatives of the throne, a very desirable attribute of the sovereign and it is also a tacit disapproval which the beneficent dispensers of public good give to the legal code whose imperfections have been propped up by the prejudices of centuries, the voluminous and imposing edifice of infinite commentaries, the grave apparatus of eternal formalities supported by the most insinuating and least feared half-educated persons. But one may consider that clemency is a virtue of the legislator and not of the administrator of the laws; that it must be reflected in the legal code, not as it is now in particular judgments; that it should show men that to pardon crimes makes punishment no longer inevitable so foments the illusion of impunity; and one is made to believe that, reprieve always being possible, sentences that are not pardoned are violent acts of force rather than justice. What will be said then, when the sovereign gives a pardon (that is, a portion of public safety) to a particular individual, which makes a private act of unenlightened beneficence into a public decree of impunity? Let the laws then be unrelenting, and the administrators of the laws unrelenting in particular cases, but let the legislator be milder, charitable, and humane. A wise architect constructs his house on a foundation of self respect—and everyone's interests amount to the general interest—so he will not be constrained at every moment by partial laws or tumultuous remedies to separate the public good from the interests of individuals or to prop up the image of public health on fear and suspicion. The profound and sensible philosopher leaves men and his brothers to enjoy in peace their portion of happiness within the immense system provided by the first Maker, He who gives them joy in this corner of the universe.]]

§ XLVII. Conclusion

I conclude with this reflection: that the severity of punishment must be relative to the state of the nation itself. It should be strongly directed at the senses if it is to impress the callous minds of a people not long out of barbarism. A thunderbolt is needed to fell a lion that merely turns toward a rifle shot. But to the extent that minds are increasingly mollified as the state of society grows in sensibility, so the force of punishment must be reduced if we wish to maintain a constant relationship between the object and the sensation.[1]

From everything that we have heretofore seen, we can construct a general theory of great utility, but one that does not conform to custom, the usual legislator of nations: *So that every punishment should not be an act of violence of one or many against a private citizen, it must be essentially public, prompt, necessary, the minimum possible in the given circumstances, in proportion to the crimes, and dictated by the laws.*

Endnotes

Title Page

Originally written in Latin, under the title "*Sermones fideles ethici, politici, oeco-nomici, sive interiora rerum*," essay n. XLV "*De officio iudici*" this is Bacon's own translation (Beirne, 1993: 24). What exactly Beccaria had in mind in using this quotation to begin his book is something of a mystery, except that it does signify his allegiance to the Scottish enlightenment thinkers whose main aim was to apply scientific principles to the study of man and society, and whose hero was Bacon. Beirne (1993: 51-52) has suggested that, in keeping with the sleight of hand often used by authors to convey hidden messages during the eighteenth century, Beccaria may have been hinting at the sentence that comes before this quotation which reads: "In dealing with cunning persons, we must ever consider their ends, to interpret their speeches; and it is good to say little to them, and that which they least look for." That is, while he has shown his allegiance to the scientific approach of the Scots (see: Introduction to the *Treatise*), he invites the reader to look for "hidden" messages in his text. Given the manner in which the *Treatise* was put together (see: Note to the Text) we doubt that Beccaria would have taken the time to fashion any subtle messages. Taken on face value, we understand the quotation simply to mean that the moderate position he takes in this text will prepare the way for greater changes. This interpretation comports with Venturi's observation of some contemporary commentators of Beccaria who argued that an immediate and complete reform of penal legislation in Europe was not to be expected, but must be perseveringly and firmly promoted (see: Francioni, 1984: 15). That said, there are many obscure passages in this *Treatise* which leave one guessing.

To the Reader

1. Beccaria wrote this note for the fifth edition, printed in Livorno by Coltellini in March, 1766 (see: Note to the Text), in response to criticisms that appeared a few months after publication of the first edition of his essay (1764). The main critic was Ferdinando Facchinei (1765), a Dominican monk from Vallombroso, who published in Venice a vitriolic booklet, *Note ed osservazioni sul libro intitolato "Dei delitti e delle pene,"* accusing the author of impiety and sedition. This section is of great interest because it is where Beccaria tries gingerly to tread the line between respect and retention of a religious view of society and human nature, but at the same time arguing for a more "detached" or what we would call today "scientific" approach to the study of law and society. The result is an often confused and difficult exposition of a crude theory of the origins and function of law. There are four elements of human life in society with which he has to grapple: religion, human nature, privilege (that is, the natural rights of sovereigns), and society (that is, the rest of us).

2. Flavius Anicius Iustinianus, known as Justinian I, the Great (483-565 A.D.), by birth a barbarian, became emperor of the Eastern Roman (Byzantine) Empire and put together the definitive consolidation of Roman law. By appointing a commission of lawyers, the most eminent of them being Tribonian, he promoted the systematization of an immense and disorganized amount of juridical material, which had accumulated over several centuries (from the law of twelve tables in 449 B.C.), from the republican times through to the empire, eventually resulting in the four books of the *Corpus iuris civilis*. This fundamental work was regarded as law in force up to the eighteenth century and provided the basis for most continental juridical systems of written laws.

3. Here Beccaria refers mainly to the customary legal practices of the Lombards, a Germanic people who invaded the northern part of Italy. A.D. 568, settling first in the Po valley and subsequently establishing a kingdom over a large portion of the country.

4. Beccaria's emphatic condemnation seems to be indiscriminately directed against the entire pre-existing juridical tradition, although soon afterwards he points out that it will be limited to criminal justice. See: note 8.

5. Benedikt Carpzov (1595-1666), professor of law at the University of Leipzig was one of the founders of German juridical science and Protestant law. His *Politica nova imperialis saxonica rerum criminalium* (1635) is considered one of the most influential criminal law treatises of the time.

6. Giulio Claro (1525-1575) Italian jurist. In the fifth book of his *Perceptae Sententiae* (1568) criminal law is conceived as a science having its own distinct principles. According to Francioni (1984: 17) his work influenced many other jurists, including Carpzov.

7. Prospero Farinacci (or Farinaccio) (1544-1618) Italian jurist and criminal lawyer, like Claro and Carpzov is placed among the founders of the new criminal law science, as an independent discipline based on Roman and Canonic law. His major work is *Praxis et theorica criminalis* (1616). He achieved great notoriety as defense attorney in the famous trial of Beatrice Cenci, later depicted by Shelley in the famous tragedy *The Cenci*. His skillful defense, however did not manage to avoid the beheading of Beatrice who was found guilty of parricide and executed in Rome, A.D. 1599.

8. These sentences could be interpreted as an attack on the common law tradition advocated and consolidated by Blackstone in England, whose commentaries were despised by Bentham (see: Introduction to the *Treatise*). The common law tradition holds as valuable the lessons learned from cases of the past. It never, if at all, took hold in Europe until late in the twentieth century.

9. *il sistema criminale*. Previous translators have translated this expression as "criminal law" or "criminal procedure." Today, we have no difficulty in translating it as "criminal justice." This term has become the most widely used term to refer to all aspects of the study of crime and the societal response to it (Benamati et al., 1997), which is in fact what Beccaria's essay is about, covering all aspects of crime and the criminal justice system (i.e., law enforcement, courts, "corrections"). It is remarkable that Beccaria referred to the application of criminal law as a "system," since it was thought at the middle of the twentieth century to be an especially modern way of describing the multiplicity of organizations, often in conflict with each other, as a "criminal justice system" (*The Challenge of Crime in a Free Society*, 1967). Later in the twentieth century, many argued that it was not a system at all, in fact that it was a non-system (Inciardi, 1984; Howard et al., 2000).

10. This laudatory comment in regard to monarchs may be read as Beccaria pandering to monarchs in order to protect himself from harm for expounding the critical views concerning the administration of criminal law (and by clear implication the making of laws). However, the beneficial views of monarchy as a type of government are recounted by Hutcheson (1755: 240-269), whose influence on Beccaria's works has been documented by Beirne (1993: 56). Hutcheson, following Montesquieu's *Spirit of Laws* (1949), claims that there are three types of government—monarchy, aristocracy, and democracy—each with its advantages and disadvantages. He concludes, generally, that a government containing elements of all three types is probably best, but certainly observes several beneficial effects of monarchical systems, which was also Montesquieu's preference.

11. Namely, the *Note ed Osservazioni* by Facchinei (1765).

12. Natural law has a long and venerable history in Western thought. It also forms the necessary basis for the emergence of social contract theory during the enlightenment. For, if natural law exists, so also does its corollary: natural rights. Thus, the social contract theories of the enlightenment were oriented to examine the rights of citizens, and in contrast the duties and obligations of the State, especially the idea that natural law through natural rights imposed limitations on the State's power. The latter was especially the view of Locke, and it was, in part, the view of Rousseau, although some commentators of his work argue that in the end, Rousseau was a totalitarian (Barker, 1947). See: Note 16 and translators' Introduction to the *Treatise* for analysis and origins of natural law. Here, Beccaria, in trying to defend himself from the religious criticism that would eventually lead to the inclusion of the *Treatise* in the *Index Librorum Prohibitorum*, presents a classic tripartite division of the sources of moral and political order (Francioni, 1984: 18, fn. 3), which is taken from Locke and Montesquieu. The *Index Librorum Prohibitorum* ("List of Prohibited Books") is a list of censored publications which the Catholic Church considers incompatible and potentially dangerous to its doctrine. Pope Paul IV promulgated the first Roman *Index* in 1577. The last thirty-second updated edition (1948), has about 4,000 titles. Almost every important modern philosopher (including Beccaria) is on the *Index*, which lists, among many others, Francis Bacon, George Berkeley, Thomas Hobbes, David Hume, Immanuel Kant, John Locke, John Stuart Mill, Montesquieu, and Jan Jacques Rousseau..

13. Thus echoing the arguments of David Hume (1748) who viewed custom as the prime mover of history, and remained a harsh critic of natural law: "Custom is that principle … so necessary to the subsistence of our species, and the regulation of our conduct, in every circumstance and occurrence of human life" (1748: 44). Hume was perhaps the most empirical of all the Scottish thinkers of the eighteenth century, demanding observable evidence of social and political claims, rejecting all supposition, especially the social contract, except the story of its origin, which he viewed as relatively unimportant, since it was what governments and societies had actually done that was the proof of how governments worked (Hume, 1999). In fact he pointed out time and again that governments were mostly formed as a result of usurpation, not by social contract. (see: Introduction to the *Treatise*.)

14. Beccaria here slips from classes of law to classes of virtue, as if they were the same. Montesquieu (1949: XIII) argued that the type of law emerges from the type of government, which in turn should be guided by its respective "virtue" (of the generic variety): Aristocratic government by moderation, monarchy by honor, democracy by virtue and despotism by fear. We see here that Montesquieu, one of the more relativistic of all the enlightenment thinkers and therefore presumably the one most likely to maintain a "value free" approach, was unable to maintain

an impartial position. He constantly mixed an "objective" analysis with value or moral judgments concerning the basis of law. This was because he held, as did probably Beccaria, an ideal view of justice: that it existed objectively over and beyond the affairs of men, societies or even deities. Unfortunately, neither he nor Beccaria consistently or clearly said exactly what they meant by "justice" although both seem to see it as something to do with moderation and equity.

15.   Following Montesquieu: "We ought not to decide by divine laws what should be decided by human laws; nor determine by human what should be determined by divine laws" (1949: XXVI, 58).

16.   Natural virtue and natural law are the great puzzlers in this section. We take natural virtue to mean the innate dispositions of men, and natural law to be the law that emerges as a result of innate dispositions that are inextricably part of Nature's order (see: Introduction to the *Treatise*). The difference between these and divine law is in one sense indistinguishable since one can argue, indeed it is usually assumed by the religious, that God preordained all elements of human nature. The Judeo-Christian tradition would argue, however, that while innate dispositions were placed by God into the human form, the expression of these dispositions in actual human behavior will vary. That is, humans are driven by God-given dispositions, but they are also guided by God-given consciousness to make choices.

17.   The insistence on three separate classes of law clearly comes from Montesquieu, whose classification of law has been termed an "ideal type" since the real world never conformed to his classification. Montesquieu identified no less than eight classes of law: law of nature, divine law, canon law, law of nations, political law, law of conquest, civil law, and domestic law, Montesquieu 1949: XXVI). He also insisted that each class of law should be studied and analyzed separately, as does Beccaria: "All beings have their laws: the Deity has His laws, the material world its laws … man his laws" (Montesquieu, 1949: I). (For a more detailed discussion of types of law and their religious and secular evolution, see: Introduction to the *Treatise*.)

18.   This reference to the famous Hobbesian precept, the war of all against all, is one of the most difficult passages in this essay. Hobbes (and many after him) imagined that a war of all against all existed among men in the primitive state of nature, before societies were formed. This idea constructed by Hobbes was not based on pure imagination (a common accusation made against him). Rather, in the society of the seventeenth century during which he wrote, he saw all around him daily evidence of hostility, war, and disorder. He lived through the turbulent period of England's civil war, perhaps the most violent period of England's colorful history. In this passage, Beccaria is trying to argue that, although men may have behaved primitively before society was born, they did so not out of innate cruelty and barbarism (the usual interpretation made by followers of Hobbes) but because they lacked guidance from God, or at least had not developed a conscious sense of the true God, and worshipped false religions. This is, therefore, a mild criticism of Hobbes, not an affirmation of his idea, though Beccaria seems to revert to the Hobbesian view later in the essay. (see: Introduction to the *Treatise* for more discussion of Hobbes and the social contract and natural law.)

19.   That is, humans possibly also contain innate dispositions that are conducive to the making of agreements with each other. One infers that Beccaria is trying to say that man may not be born a violent savage, but may instead have a cooperative nature. Here, he follows closely the thinking of the Scots, especially Hutcheson and his student Ferguson, who argued simply that man was innately a "social animal" (Bryson, 1945). Here also his view of the social contract comes closer to that of

Rousseau (1947), which is properly defined as a contract of society, or mutual association of individuals, who make no contract with the State (as they do in Hobbes's *Leviathan*). The coming together of free individuals for Rousseau is one in which their association forms a general will. The complexities of Rousseau's theory of the social contract are examined more closely in the Introduction to the *Treatise*.

20. *Pubblicista*, from the French *"publiciste,"* an expert of public law, especially of theory of the State.

21. However, we may ask at this point, does "political" include the behavior of the government? We note that, after paying homage to the sovereign and legislators in the first paragraph ("kind and enlightened government"), there has been no reference to their role in creating or administering law. Yet Beccaria is clearly arguing that it is the political sphere that is the most important in the study of the creation and administration of criminal law. If one takes away the sovereign and legislators, what is left for the political sphere? It leaves those on the "front line" of criminal justice as we would term them today, namely the judges and others concerned with law enforcement, neither of which makes laws.

22. The *Reply to Notes and Observations* (*Risposta ad uno scritto che s'intitola Note ed osservazioni sul libro "Dei delitti e delle pene,"*) was entirely written by the Verri brothers, particularly by Pietro and was added to the third edition (1765) of the *Treatise*. Beccaria took complete credit for the *Reply* and did not acknowledge the Verri's input in the production of the *Treatise*, thus provoking their resentment, resulting in a definitive and permanent break between them in 1766 (see: Newman and Marongiu, 1990: 331-332; see also Note to the Text).

23. Tiresome though it may be to have one's basic premises constantly questioned, this is surely what all scholars should do in analysis of any serious text. In this case, however, Beccaria puts up a smoke screen by railing against the religious fanatics who assailed him. In fact, the basic premises of his approach were never directly questioned: those of the social contract, and the entrenched utilitarian idea of the greatest happiness for the greatest number, the received truth of eighteenth-century enlightenment.

Introduction

1. This sentence is almost identical to one of Pietro Verri's (1766: 84), who in his *Meditazioni sulla felicità* (first published in 1763), wrote: *La legislazione peggiore di tutte è quella dove i doveri e i diritti di ogni uomo sono incerti e confusi e la felicità condensata in pochi, lasciando nella miseria i molti* ("The worst of all legislation is the one in which everyone's duties and rights are uncertain and confused and happiness is concentrated among the few, leaving the many in misery"—our translation).

2. See the Introduction to the *Treatise* for a more extensive consideration of the different theories of the social contract and relationship to natural law.

3. *freddo esaminatore*. Sometimes translated as "detached examination." This is, of course the core ideal of science. The idea of science applied to the study of human social arrangements, that is sociology, was in its infancy in the eighteenth century. But this is exactly what Beccaria was getting at in this introduction, and of course his quotation from Francis Bacon at the beginning of the book makes clear his commitment to the scientific approach.

4. The word happiness, of course, is a most useful word for Beccaria, as it was to most of the eighteenth-century philosophers. He never attempted to define it, and it is used in many different senses throughout the book. Given Beccaria's advocacy

of direct punishments that impact the senses (see the following section) it is likely that he was assuming a version of the pleasure/pain principle (men are motivated by the avoidance of pain and pursuit of pleasure). This assumption underlying the greatest happiness formula was made very explicit in Bentham's utilitarian theories (Bentham, 1948), who also turned the idea into a specific formula: the "felific calculus."

5.   *in diviso* (*la massima felicità divisa nel maggior numero*). Beccaria transforms the value assertion of the social contract into this utilitarian formula, subsequently made famous by the English philosopher Jeremy Bentham, a great admirer of Beccaria's *Treatise*. There is also some argument as to the correct translation of this sentence, since the Italian superlatives are slightly different: "*massimo*" meaning "the greatest" and "*maggiore*" meaning "the greater." Thus, strictly speaking it should read "the greatest happiness for the greater number." We think that the difference is slight, though it does point up one of the hidden difficulties in this wonderful sounding utilitarian dictum: whether we use "greatest or "greater" both imply that not everyone can be included in the greatest happiness.

6.   This brief mention of change reveals much. It suggests one small way in which Beccaria diverges from Montesquieu, who, while he saw that nations did things differently, would most likely not have ascribed to them the ability to control their own destinies to the extent that they could hasten up the progress of history. However, of great interest here is the idea that societies go through stages, and that there is an inevitability that they will progress though these stages ultimately to reach a condition of enlightenment and even perfection. The conceptual problem was that, if one posits a normal development of humanity (fixed by God, by the way) why is it that there are such wide differences in development? Their answers, including that of Aristotle, were simply that "errors" or "accidents" occurred along the way to interfere with the normal rate of progress (Bock, 1978: 39-75). Thus, Beccaria uses the words *combinazioni e vicissitudini umane*, accidents and human foibles, to explain the delay in progress.

7.   This is probably a reference to Hutcheson (1725) who termed himself an "obscure Philosopher" and whose utilitarian ideas heavily influenced Beccaria (Beirne, 1993: 28). However, it is doubtful that Beccaria had Hutcheson in mind in the previous sentence (in fact the reference is more probably to Helvétius), as the Scottish Enlightenment thinkers were not especially impressed by the French ideas of progress. In fact Beccaria openly acknowledged Helvétius' influence in a 1766 letter to André Morellet (the French translator and editor of the *Treatise* in which he writes: "I owe to the reading of *L'Esprit* most of my ideas" (see: Francioni, 1984: 24, fn. 1).

8.   *Stampa.* We use that especially modern expression of the twenty-first century, "news media" to translate this word. Of course there was no television or radio in Beccaria's time. There was a flourishing printing trade, but many public lectures took the dissemination of ideas even further (Ewen, 1988). In addition, the dissemination of ideas via the print media could not have occurred without a matching improvement in communications, especially through transportation and trade. *Stampa* has taken on a much broader meaning in Italy of the twenty-first century.

9.   Quite a few of Beccaria's other (less distinguished) writings were on economics. This passage has an almost modern ring to it, presaging Adam Smith's inquiry into the wealth of nations, published just twelve years after the *Treatise*, in which Smith argues that the free pursuit of individual self interest through open markets and competition is a major builder of wealth (read happiness) for all (Smith, 1976).

Smith was an active member of the Scottish enlightenment thinkers, which included Hutcheson, one of his teachers, Hume and Locke all of whom have influenced Beccaria's writings to some degree (see: Introduction to the *Treatise*).

10.   It is uncertain what Beccaria means by "errors" since we understand this word as a mistake of some kind, usually resulting from a bad decision or choice. However, it may well be that Beccaria was thinking in a broad historical sense, that certain events in history reflected human error. The "accumulated errors" to which Beccaria refers are essentially the man-made circumstances in society that appear to repress human endeavor.

11.   Indeed, as Montesquieu touched lightly on many subjects. The father of modern sociology, Emile Durkheim viewed Montesquieu as having invented the field of sociology.

12.   To distinguish Beccaria's approach from that of Montesquieu is in fact very difficult, largely because Beccaria's references to Montesquieu are oblique, and rarely direct, although Montesquieu is the only enlightenment philosopher referred to by name in the entire book. There is a hint in this passage of one difference, and that is in their theory of history. According to Montesquieu, history was the product of macro forces; it could not be changed by individuals. Beccaria seems here to believe that maybe special individuals could change its course (see Introduction to the *Treatise*).

§ I. The Origin of Punishments

1.   That the social contract and utilitarian theories form the solid foundation on which much of Beccaria's theory of punishment and law stands, is very clear. The idea that the pursuit of public utility is one important reason for the creation of the social contract, for instance, was already present in Grotius' view of natural law (see: the Introduction to the *Treatise*). What is not clear is which version of the social contract he adheres to. We have reviewed the different versions of the social contract in our introduction to the text. For now, it suffices to say that this passage appears to adopt the Hobbes version, indicated by his claim that the "contract of society" (i.e., individuals depositing their portion of liberty for the common good) is legitimately owned by the sovereign (i.e., there is no "contract of government," and the Leviathan or State assumes ownership of the public good without consent). Other interpreters of Beccaria argue that he adheres to the Lockean view of social contract, that it was established as a result of private property which involved a contract of government. This legitimized the government to enforce law in exchange for protecting individuals' property. It is not clear from this passage whether Beccaria also had in mind Rousseau's idea of the "general will" which was supposed to be more than just the sum of each individual will (see further, Introduction to the *Treatise*).

2.   *Sensibili motivi*. We have translated this term as "concrete incentives" given that in a few sentences later, Beccaria makes it very clear that these punishments must directly strike the senses. Possibly, a closer translation could be "concrete deterrents," but this expression is too close to the word "punishment" a word used sparingly in this section, which is surprising since the section is about the origin of punishment. We use the word "concrete" because it more closely suggests that words are not enough. Actions, probably those that have a visible and physical effect on the offender are essential to achieve the order that Beccaria, on behalf of the social contract, is concerned to preserve. Does he mean corporal punishment? Not necessarily, but this section does appear to rule out the use of "talking cures" that we know of today. In this section, Beccaria clearly is persuaded that only

strong and direct punishments are enough to keep a society that is composed of warlike individuals under control. This is a surprising opening to a book that is widely known for advocating milder punishments.

3. What are we to conclude from this section about the origin of punishment? Beccaria's answer is simple and traditional: it lies in the violent disposition of human nature. If individuals did not break the laws, punishments would not be necessary. Unfortunately, according to Beccaria, individuals are naturally constituted to break the laws, indeed, they are even driven to break the laws. And ironically, according to this version of the social contract, law breakers must be punished in order to preserve the society in which individuals have a heavy stake, yet also are strongly disposed to usurp. There appears to be no exit from this theoretical circle.

§ II. The Right to Punish

1. See Montesquieu ((1949: passim) and note 1, chapter I).
2. A similar version of mankind's development can be found both in Montesquieu and Rousseau (see: Francioni, 1984: 31, fn. 4), and Introduction to the *Treatise*.
3. Beccaria's notion here of a minimal and involuntary surrendering of individual liberty is closer to Helvétius' and Locke's view than Rousseau's. See: Introduction to the *Treatise* and Chapter I.

§ III. Implications So Far

1. Beccaria here reflects the now common idea of the "rule of law" as it is widely recognized today. Beccaria throughout the book refers constantly to the theory of law that proposes that law results from the agreements made among free men, that is, the social contract. This places him in the camp of what today theorists in criminology and sociology of law refer to as "consensus theory." It is only a theory, though, but one can see throughout that Beccaria treats it as both fact and value. He also claims that laws are dominated by the powerful, which puts him in the camp of the conflict theorists (Bernard, 1983; Vold and Bernard, 1986).
2. The first modern theory of separation of powers was that of Montesquieu in *De l'Esprit des Lois* (originally published in 1748). Here Beccaria seems particularly concerned with the necessity for a clear separation between legislative and judiciary powers. The concept that liberty is most effectively protected by the separation of powers, however, was already present in Locke's writings and in the English Constitution.
3. That is, the "greatest number."
4. See, again, Montesquieu and Rousseau (Francioni, 1984: 35, fn. 1).

§ IV. The Interpretation of Laws

1. *Obbligazione... giuramento.* This passage is widely mistranslated because of its convoluted grammatical construction. The word *giuramento* takes on considerable significance here. Beccaria, anticipating Freud by more than one hundred years, suggests that the willing choice to obey is rooted in the primitive feeling of slavish obedience to a powerful leader and/or custom. He calls it an "oath" but he clearly implies that it reflects a deep seated sentiment, so deep that it is physical in nature.. This is a conception of human psychology that assumes a progression from the "primitive" (driven solely by instinct) to the "civilized" where the minds of men are, although at bottom driven by instinct (Freud), nevertheless sufficiently rational

as to make it possible to choose obedience to society because they see that what is good for society is also in their own interests. It is summed up as a physical (*fisico*) feeling of obligation, later in the twentieth century to be expressed in a new form, a feeling of "solidarity" as in Marx's theory of communism.

2. Which means arbitrariness. This entire section summarizes Beccaria's well known position against judicial discretion and in favor of a literal application of the law, directly taken from Montesquieu (1949: book VI, 3 and XI, 6).

3. This passage offers a strikingly similar assessment of "democracy" to the later well known observations of America made by Tocqueville (1899) based on his visit to America in 1831.

§ V. The Obscurity of the Laws

1. That is, if laws are interpreted by insiders who are separated from ordinary people, the humanity of these laws will be distant from the interests of ordinary men and the laws will quickly lose their relevance to peoples' needs as time moves on.

2. *Passioni*: Philosophical tradition has often considered human passions (a wider notion which includes emotions), as having a negative and destructive influence on the soul or mind. The religious view on this subject has often associated passions with sin, therefore prescribing their strict repression and control. Probably, in this context the meaning is that of emotions, as opposed to reason and thus capable of inducing irrational response.

§ VI. The Proportion between Crime and Punishment

1. *Spinte*. In modern terminology, we might, in this context, call this the offender's motivation, except that there is considerable difficulty in deciding whether Beccaria meant that the offender was pushed to complete his crime (motivation, instinct, drive, etc.), or pulled or induced to commit the crime by external conditions (provoked, invoked, into action). The former assumes an internal state of the offender, the latter assumes that factors external to the individual determine the outcome of the act. Furthermore, the next sentence refers to how difficult it is to control human passions, which presumably are internal states of mankind. Bentham's highly complex theory of the "springs to action" (1789) would later develop this idea of internal motivation.

2. Montesquieu, in his *Spirit of Laws*, Book VI, Chapter XVI (Of the just Proportion between Punishments and Crimes), writes: "It is an essential point, that there should be a certain proportion in punishments, because it is essential that a great crime should be avoided rather than a smaller, and that which is more pernicious to society rather than that which is less."

3. There appears to be a contradiction here, or at least it is unclear what Beccaria has in mind. The problem is the vagueness of the concept "national sentiment." If it decreases, one would have thought that public interest in crime would decrease. However, Beccaria is saying that interest in crime increases because crime increases. So, there must be other public sentiments that Beccaria has in mind that are different from "national sentiment." These are, presumably, the human passions that drive men to punish (though not stated by Beccaria) which are possibly identical to those that drive men to crime. In the next paragraph Beccaria attempts to say what this force is. But it is not until the next chapter that he begins to link the classic Benthamite pleasure and pain to crime and punishment.

4. That is the "concrete incentives" (*sensibili motivi*): see Chapter I.

5. This appears to be a *non sequitur*, unless Beccaria explains how conflicts between private interests lead to a scale of disorders. Adam Smith, for example, sees conflicts among private interests (competition) as producing wealth and happiness.
6. See: Helvétius, on the variability of moral ideas (Francioni, 1984: 43, fn. 1).
7. This sentence is taken directly from Helvétius (Ibid., fn. 2). However, the pleasure-pain hedonistic principle can be traced back to the epicurean tradition. See, obviously, Bentham (1789), Marongiu and Newman (1997), Newman and Marongiu (1997).
8. Helvétius, Ibid., page 44, fn. 1.

§ VII. Errors in the Measurement of Crime

1. This chapter title is a little misleading, though it does anticipate the modern social science attempts to measure crime. It is not about measuring the extent of crime as criminologists do when they collect crime statistics. Rather, it addresses the question of the comparative gravity or seriousness of crime. This may or may not be a measurement problem, and indeed was until the twentieth century considered mainly a legal problem. It was not until the work of Sellin and Wolfgang (1964) that the seriousness of crime was treated as a problem of empirical measurement.
2. This view on the assessment of the gravity of crime, which considers only the harm done to society, is different from most modern legal traditions which also take into account criminal intent (*mens rea*). The approach was extended by Barbara Wooton (1959) in her utilitarian justification for the social defense school of punishment, that is, punishment must match only the harm done to society (and sometimes to the victim), the offender's state of mind being irrelevant. This view of crime is found in many modern statutes that incorporate "strict liability" in various traffic offenses and in other regulatory areas of law such as the regulation of health and human safety in the workplace. Beccaria here seems to advocate the application of strict liability to all crime, an extreme position by today's standards. Yet in the following chapter he seems not to take this extreme position.

§ VIII. The Classification of Crimes

1. These are the prejudices of despotism, typical according to Montesquieu and Hélvetius, of oriental regimes. However Beccaria's argument here is against the existing western juridical tradition.
2. This is an unsatisfactory reason. In fact, given that Beccaria has rejected even the slightest semblance of judicial discretion in interpreting the laws, it is surely necessary for legislators to define in detail every single crime and circumstance—an impossibility of course. See also note 6 below and the Introduction to the *Treatise*, especially in regard to Bentham who attempted such an exhaustive classification.
3. This general division of crimes is very similar to Montesquieu's classification (1949: book XII, 4).
4. High treason.
5. Legal codes of today still face this problem. The cavalier distinction between felonies and misdemeanors for example lumps an incredible variety of crimes into just two baskets, resulting in grossly disproportionate punishments for many crimes that are called misdemeanors—disproportionate, that is, if one measures their gravity only by the harm done to society as Beccaria argues.
6. This is one of Beccaria's more impenetrable sentences. He seems to be saying that there is an eternal truth (which defies mystification) that is immutably separated from the observable and recurring relationships among men and society.

§ IX. Honor

1.   This sentence is taken directly from Verri's *Meditazioni sulla felicità*. (1766). See: Francioni (1984: 50, fn. 2).

2.   *Opinione* Other translators translate this word directly as "opinion" but it is difficult to interpret this word because of its widespread use in everyday English, particularly as "public opinion," which presumably Beccaria did not mean, since it assumes a widespread exchange of ideas among the "public" which had not yet formed at the very early period in societal history imagined by Beccaria. For this reason we here translate *opinione* as "primitive beliefs" following Durkheim's idea of the elementary forms of religious life. Our translation is supported by the next two sentences in which Beccaria is arguing that there was a movement, ever so elementary, towards solidarity among individuals that superseded or was more effective than laws. This is a fascinating idea which seems to suggest that the ability to form the basis of the social contract came before laws held sway in society and in this passage even implies that there was even in the early origins of society a split between law and society; that the law could not achieve for men the security that they wanted. As the rest of this paragraph indicates, though, it turns out that the elementary beliefs are not true—that is, they are religious, though Beccaria does not say so, probably because he fears reprimand from the church. Much of his argument here parallels Voltaire's well known cynical view of religion as a divisor of society, working against the common interest. Thus, there is a glimmer in Beccaria's thinking here that anticipates Durkheim's theory of the elementary forms of religious life, though Durkheim saw them as having a more positive bonding function, a clear and positive step towards the progression to a more sophisticated "civilized" society. While Beccaria here sees the idea of honor as a backward step (indeed working against the social bond), he nevertheless sees that society is moving towards a more civilized state, through a series of stages to a more perfect state This is why he later refers to the backward step as "temporary."

3.   That is, the rights of individual men as individuals, not as rights of citizens in society. Thus, honor serves to protect the individual, but not the individual in society.

4.   Foucault (1977) two centuries later would take up this analogy to the sovereign to explain how the violent and public punishments common up to and around Beccaria's time were reflections of the direct relationship of the common people to the sovereign in whose person was located all power and authority and thus the only source of social order. By Foucault's reckoning, Beccaria's time was not much different from the almost primitive state that Beccaria is here describing.

5.   That is, the war of all against all where all were "equal" in the state of nature, but none were secure so that equality had no value.

§ XI. Disturbing the Peace

1.   After those threatening societal order and those against life and personal safety, here Beccaria takes into account "minor" crimes.

2.   Here Beccaria seems to advocate the general principle of legality for police practice.

3.   Presumably Beccaria means the individual human rights promoted by the *Philosophes*, especially in the Declaration of the rights of man, which Bentham viewed with derision. See: Horowitz (1954: 186-187).

§ XII. Disturbing the Peace

1.   See Francioni (1984: 55, fn.1)

§ XIII. On Witnesses

1.   Civil death is a term that refers to the loss of all or almost all civil rights of a person due to a conviction for a serious crime and it is usually inflicted on persons convicted of crimes against the state. Historically, outlawry, that is, declaring a person as an outlaw was a common form of civil death, since the outlaw could be killed with impunity by anyone.
2.   Thus, the credibility of witnesses in accusations of sorcery is extremely low. See: Montesquieu (1949: XII, 5).
3.   Here probably Beccaria refers to threats or criminal designs as reported in a trial.

§ XIV. Evidence and Forms of Judgment

1.   This appears to contradict the many other places where Beccaria has praised the scientific approach to understanding and governing society. It is even more difficult to reconcile this statement with Beccaria's clear rejection of judicial discretion, where he insists that the only way to overcome this is to issue precise and detailed laws for the judge to follow without question. This seems to suggest that law should in fact be reduced to a set of scientifically derived statements. Beccaria may mean here that judges issue their discretionary legal decisions as though they had the authority of scientific rules, and that, when the law is not as clear as it should be, the interpretation is better left to common sense rather than to the "scientific" wisdom of the judge.

§ XV. Secret Accusations

1.   Here Beccaria refers to the extensive practice of espionage and secret accusations in the Republic of Venice. See: Francioni (1984: 60, fn. 1).

§ XVI. Torture

1.   This argument is taken directly from Verri (see: Francioni, 1984: 63, fn. 2). It has been noted that all the information and arguments of this very famous chapter are expounded, with a detailed indication of the sources used, in Verri's *Osservazioni sulla tortura.*. This book, although published only in 1804, was most probably already available to Beccaria in a draft version when he was working on the *Treatise*. The very image of the torture as a "crucible" in which the guilty is purged of his infamy is also Verri's (see: Venturi, 1999: 132).
2.   See note below on how Beccaria's affirmation of general deterrence undermines his main argument in this chapter.
3.   That is the fire of Purgatory.
4.   That is, the normal cause-effect relationship is supposedly interrupted by divine intervention during the so-called *Judgments of God*.
5.   Strictly speaking this is almost true. Because of the common law structure of English criminal justice, the infliction of pain on an offender could not be administered until after the finding of guilt. However, there was one exception to this which was the practice of pressing (*peine forte et dure*) (Newman, 2008),

imported probably from France, and applied to an offender who refused to plead (that is, plead guilt or innocence at the beginning of his trial). Pressing involved the placing of heavy weights on the accused as he lay flat on the ground under a board until the accused submitted his plea. This is a much more simplified and restricted utilitarian use of pain, but utilitarian none the less. Beccaria's larger point however is valid. Tortures of the kind used in the rest of Europe were never adopted in England, probably because of England's common law system. Nasty forms of the death penalty were however widespread in England in the seventeenth century and before as they were in Europe.

6. Adolf Frederik of Sweden put an end to judicial torture for ordinary crimes in 1734, but it was not until 1772 that it was totally abolished by Gustavus III.

7. That is Frederick II, King of Prussia, a prominent exponent of so-called "enlightened despotism." During his reign he promoted a number of reforms, including an important legislative modernization with a new Code, the "Frederician code." He abolished judicial torture in 1740.

8. This is an impressive and persuasive debating point. However, its power rests on a significant omission in this essay which is that Beccaria nowhere defines the word "punishment." This has led later scholars to misinterpret Beccaria as having opposed corporal punishment, which he did not. See Chapter XX (Violent Crimes): "Some crimes are assaults on persons others on possessions. The former should be infallibly punished with corporal punishments." Also in Chapter XXII (Theft): ."…when theft is mixed with violence, likewise the penalty should be a mixture of corporal punishment and penal servility." Scholars since Beccaria have established a standard definition of punishment which includes: (1) It must be an intentional infliction of pain (2) for an offence against a rule (3) inflicted by a person other than the offender (4) inflicted on the offender who broke the rule. Clearly, any infliction of pain on an individual whose infraction has not been proved is not punishment—though it may be something else, such as torture. In this chapter Beccaria establishes the meaning of torture as intentional pain inflicted on an accused in order to achieve other ends, mainly a confession or other incriminating details. This is a utilitarian definition of torture and the one that is mostly subscribed to by modern scholars. The infliction of pain in direct proportion to an offense—that is to match the crime with the punishment—expresses a retributive theory of punishment which eschews inflicting pain for any utilitarian purpose, and argues only that a punishment should be inflicted on an individual if his offense deserves it. See Newman (1983).

9. This last sentence seems to weaken the rest of this very powerful chapter against torture, because it is paradoxically based on a critique of the utilitarian use of pain to establish guilt. Here, Beccaria appears to affirm the utility of punishment as a general deterrent, he underwrites the utilitarian justification for punishment which, taken logically, leads to a justification for punishment (or threatening punishment) against individuals who have not yet committed a crime. That is, the intentional infliction of pain on those who are innocent, which is, by his own definition, torture.

§ XVII. Revenue Authorities

1. This chapter is really about the judge's official acting as a debt collector for the crown or sovereign and the implications this utilitarian role has for the criminal justice process. It says little about financial crimes and even less about financial punishments, which today we would interpret as meaning fines and/or reparations.

2.   This is a sweeping generalization that does not stand the test of history. Depending on what place in Europe and in what period, financial (or equivalent) ways of an offender making reparations for his crimes, including violent crimes, may or may not have dominated (Newman, 2008). It is more likely that financial reparations occurred in periods when there was a weak ruler, where feuding factions had worked out ways to deal with their own differences without interference of a third party. Even here, though, blood feuds also existed side by side with the use of financial reparations (Marongiu and Newman, 1987: 71-74).

3.   Since here Beccaria explicitly refers to "criminal procedures of every part of enlightened Europe in the eighteenth century," we should assume that the distinction between offensive and informative proceeding reflects the well known distinction between an *inquisitorial* and *adversarial* (or *accusatory*) legal system. In an *inquisitorial* system an investigating magistrate or judge is actively involved in determining the facts of the case, as opposed to an adversarial system where the role of the court is solely that of an impartial referee between parties. *Inquisitorial* systems in Beccaria's time were used in most countries of continental Europe, including Italy. In England, however, at least since the time of King Henry II (twelfth century) the secular common law operated under the *adversarial* system, still generally adopted in common law countries. The adversarial principle that a person could not be tried until formally accused is also embedded in article 38 of the *Magna Carta* (1215): "No bailiff for the future shall, upon his own unsupported complaint, put anyone to his law, without credible witnesses brought for this purpose."

§ XIX. Prompt Punishment

1.   Here Beccaria states the basic utilitarian views on general deterrence and on punishment as a necessary evil. See: Newman (2008).

2.   The conception of the intellect as a "fabric" is taken from Bacon. The idea that it is based on the association of ideas is taken from Hume, Locke and Condillac (see: Francioni: 71, fn. 1).

3.   That is, only few superior men, impassionedly striving after a distant ideal, are able to ignore the more immediate sensations and ideas compelling vulgar men to action. Having argued earlier that it is ideas (rational thoughts) that bind men's minds to their sensations, Beccaria here introduces a basic theory of how the civilized or sophisticated mind is able to delay gratification (to use Freudian terminology) for more important, perhaps intellectual goals, which are quite distant from immediate satisfaction of pleasures. See: Newman (2008) for a discussion of the Freudian basis of punishment theory.

4.   In other words, he affirms the old retributive principle that the punishment should fit the crime, though with a utilitarian twist. Retribution is widely seen in the literature as the opposite to the utilitarian justification for punishment, and generally speaking this is true. However, it is not completely true, as retribution may be used for utilitarian purposes. See: Newman (2008).

§ XX. Violent Crimes

1.   A very important point stating clearly that violent crime should be punished with (possibly violent) corporal punishment, since we have just been told that the punishment must fit the crime. This seems to run against his argument for the mildness of punishments.

2.   That is, extinguish these kinds of crimes with fines or pecuniary compensation.

§ XXI. Punishing Nobles

1. The nobles and the clergy in Beccaria's time were entitled to numerous legal privileges. It can be said that their juridical status was largely different from the other social classes. They were subject to trial in special tribunals and received, except in special cases, milder and usually pecuniary punishments.
2. On the intermediary function of the nobility between the king and the populace see Montesquieu, (1949: II, 4).
3. This very long sentence states Beccaria's position on inequality: the only acceptable inequality should derive from differences in terms of personal abilities, thus favoring social mobility, instead of perpetuation of privileges according to heredity.
4. See, again on the origins of social contract, Introduction to the *Treatise*.

§ XXII. Theft

1. This chapter is remarkable in its use of the classic, and very old, method of matching punishments to crimes according to their qualitative attributes, in this case very similar to Dante's methodology. The offender is subjected to punishments that match the sin or immorality of the offence. Thus, a thief must be made poor. And later in this chapter, a violent thief must be subjected to violence through corporal punishment and forced labor. There is little here that expresses the utilitarian notion of punishment advocated throughout the *Treatise*, except to extrapolate using Dante, that reflecting the crime in the punishment is an excellent teacher, a way to cleanse the soul. See: Newman (2008).
2. It should be noted that Beccaria in the first edition of the *Treatise* (Livorno, 1764) wrote "terrible *but necessary right*, changing it to "terrible *and perhaps unnecessary right*" in the third edition (Lausanna, 1765). Elsewhere in this edition of the *Treatise*, he refers to the "sacred ownership of property," though stating, in the same chapter that "commerce and private property are not a goal of the social contract, but can be a means to obtain it" (see: Chapter XXXIV on Debtors). So it is difficult to establish his position on the right of property, According to Francioni (1984: 75, fn. 3) Beccaria's more radical view derives from Rousseau.
3. The innocent members of the offender's family.
4. That is, prison and forced labor. Blackstone cited with approval Beccaria's advocacy of this punishment for theft, comparing it to the dominant historical punishment of death. Interestingly, Blackstone, perhaps mistakenly, calls this punishment a type of corporal punishment (Blackstone, 1853: 191).
5. Corporal punishment and forced labor, often at the time amounting to a form of aggravated death penalty.
6. That is, it is impossible to make comparisons between things of a different nature, such as robbery and theft.

§ XXIII. Public Condemnation

1. Which, of course, implies a loss of personal honor. Here Beccaria continues to parallel Dante's method of matching punishments to the quality of the crime, and to link this notion to a universal morality, which, of course, was expressed in Dante's trilogy that gave credence to the then Roman Catholic views on punishment and sin in the hereafter.
2. Beccaria here appears to use the word "infamy" as synonymous with "public condemnation." Modern usage might prefer "public shaming."

3.   Again, Beccaria urges the use of "conceit against conceit" and "force against force," classic biblical terminology that is retributive rather than utilitarian, except that Beccaria makes clear that this method of punishment is of more utility *because* it is retributive. See: Newman (2008).

§ XXIV. Political Indolence

1.   It should be noted that nowhere in this chapter does Beccaria clearly indicate who these parasites are. However probably his attack is against the monastic contemplative orders, and so interpreted and fiercely criticized by Facchinei in his *Note ed ossservazioni* (1765: 79-88). That such parasites should be punished at all, let alone by banishment, by today's standards seems to be a direct assault on an individual's liberty and "free speech," given that Beccaria disapproves of the strong and perhaps persuasive opinions of the indolent. Beccaria's utopian idea of liberty based on the social contract as an essentially utilitarian mechanism leads to his conclusion that those not useful to society should be excluded from it. In other words, among other things, there is no room for dissent. This is the dark side of the utilitarian society, the precursor of Orwell's *1984*.

§ XXV. Banishment and Confiscation

1.   In Beccaria's time the law prescribed a total submission to the head of the family. Beccaria was understandably sensitive to this problem, since his father, not approving his son's marriage with Teresa Blasco, cut them both off, allowing them very little money. See: Maestro (1973: 6-8).

§ XXVI. On the Spirit of the Family

1.   That is: while the father is still alive he rules everything; after his death, the law allows personal independence and, above all, the heirs inherit his patrimony.
2.   The idea of a basic opposition between State and family interest is probably taken from Bacon and Rousseau. See: Francioni (1984: 82, fn. 1, 2, 3). Caso (1975: 25), Beccaria's ardent admirer, speculates that this passage helped frame the opening phrase that introduced the American Constitution with "We, the People" chosen after considerable debate with some who wanted "We, the States…"
3.   Lucius Cornelius Silla, Dictator of Rome from 82 to 79 B.C. is well known for his cruelty, ambition, and support of absolutism.

§ XXVII. The Mildness of Punishments

1.   This is a central point of the utilitarian theory of punishment. Recall, however, that such a theory does not necessarily advocate mild punishments. See: Newman (2008) and Introduction to the *Treatise*.
2.   This refers to the avarice and weakness of corrupted judges.
3.   Given its long and dreadful history, this assertion is doubtful indeed. Depending on the period and country, offenders were spread-eagled on the spokes of a wheel, and the major bones of their bodies broken with a large club. Other means of breaking on the wheel have included rolling the unfortunate offender down a hill, trussed to the edge or bottom of the wheel. See: Newman (2008). Beccaria also seems to assume that the punishment of prison came before the wheel, which is

also probably not correct. Prison, as a widespread punishment is a comparatively recent punishment. Breaking on the wheel is one of the oldest.
4. See: Montesquieu (1901).
5. See: Montesquieu (1949).
6. Beccaria did, however, believe that crime and punishment were in fact connected through cause and effect, a belief based on the associationism of Hume (1739) and Helvétius (1758). This was the claim that ideas were mental images, essentially sensations, which were connected through the recognition of their basic similarity; similar to the physical world where like attracts like either in time or space. "It is well established that the association of ideas is the cement that shapes the whole structure of the human intellect; without it, pleasure and pain would be isolated feelings with no consequences" (quoted in Beirne, 1993: 804). See also note 5, Chapter XXXVIII.
7. In this dense and moving passage, Beccaria describes the procedures used by the Holy Inquisition against those accused of heresy.

§ XXVIII. The Punishment of Death

1. See: Chapter I, fn. 1 on the contractual origin of law and sovereignty.
2. Roman citizens enjoyed the highest status and rights (*status civitatis*) in Roman society and could not, except under exceptional circumstances, be deprived of citizenship. As a general rule, a Roman citizen could not be sentenced to death, nor to judicial torture for any crime but treason and, even if convicted of this crime, could not be subjected to humiliating forms of execution (like crucifixion), but rather (more honorably) beheaded. However there is historical evidence of exceptions to this rule since Roman citizens have been put to death in other ways than decapitation (Cantarella, 1991: 189). Also, Romans could hardly be cited as an example of opposition to the death penalty, since they were well known in antiquity for their extensive application of dreadful and peculiar punishments. The atrocious torment of the "sack" (*poena cullei*), was, for instance, reserved for parricides. They were sewn alive into a leather sack (to symbolize the womb the parricide violated by killing a parent) along with an ape, a dog, a viper and a rooster and then drowned. Indeed, sadism appears to be a distinctive feature of ancient Roman culture, and there have been speculations about its role in the development as well as in the decline of Roman society. For an in-depth account and analysis of the forms and meaning of execution in ancient Rome, see: Cantarella (1991: 119-438).
3. Elizaveta Petrovna (1709-1761), the daughter of Peter the Great of Russia, reigned from 1741 to 1761. She abolished the death penalty with two decrees, promulgated in 1753 and 1754. It has been noted, however (Beccaria, 1999: 118, fn. 71), that in fact capital punishment was simply replaced with harsh corporal penalties, chiefly with the *knut*, a severe whipping procedure (up to 400 strokes) which frequently led to the death of the subject, who, in case of survival, was usually deported to slave labor colonies in Siberia (which in fact simply amounted to a delayed form of execution, given the awfully harsh living conditions in such colonies).. Branding on the forehead and cheeks and tearing off nostrils was also common. So, it is difficult to see how this Empress could be credited for introducing a more lenient penal legislation in her country.
4. These are the Persians and Spartans. Beccaria here cites the former as an example of wicked and subjugated people and the latter as brave and free ones.
5. Like Condillac, Helvétius took a radical empiricist position, that man was born a *tabula rasa* and formed his knowledge from the senses and association of ideas.

All man's faculties and human understanding may thus be reduced to physical sensation, even memory and judgment. This radical empiricist school of thought is known as "sensationism." The repeatedly asserted view that impressions should be more frequent rather than intense in order to be effective is taken form *De l'esprit*, particularly book III (see Francioni, 1984: 90, fn. 2).

6. Strictly speaking, if Beccaria means "intensity" rather than, "severity" (which would include both intensity and duration) he is confused about what intense pain is, since perpetual slavery is not intense, although it is long.

7. This famous passage has been often cited by Beccaria's detractors to reveal his real attitude towards extremely harsh (rather than mild) punishments. One would add that such an attitude is totally consistent with a utilitarian and instrumental conception of punishment.

8. Leading a band of few men.

9. That is, from the point of view of the assassinated person there is less pain, provided that such a person has no anticipation of being murdered.

10. These sentences do not seem to answer satisfactorily the question Beccaria claims to have answered. His problem is that he cannot acknowledge the contradiction in his argument throughout the *Treatise*: that man's nasty human nature is so nasty it can't be overcome with words, even his! See the Introduction to the *Treatise*.

11. Here Beccaria refers to three Roman Emperors of the I and II century AD who enjoyed a reputation for being concerned for the needs of the common Roman people. Titus Flavius Vespasianus, or Titus (30-81 A.D.; Emperor, 79-81 A.D. was an efficient administrator. He started a vast building program, constructing The Flavian Amphitheater, or Coliseum, and new imperial baths nearby. Titus was well known for his generosity and geniality. During his brief reign Rome's financial situation improved. Titus is also remembered for implementing legislative measures, especially in favour of the veterans. Marcus Ulpius Traianius, or Trajan (53-117 A.D. Emperor, 98-117 A.D.) devoted much of his effort to Rome's infrastructure. His greatest achievement in the city was the forum (*Forum Traianum*), the largest "imperial fora." On top of Nero's *Domus Aurea*, on the Esquiline, he constructed colossal imperial baths and a new sixty kilometers aqueduct from Lake Bracciano to Rome. His hexagonal harbour at Ostia was the most important port in Italy, making it easy to ship the grain up the Tiber to Rome. Marcus Aurelius Antoninus, or Antoninus *Pious* (86-161 A.D.; Emperor, 138-161 A.D.) has been described as a man of moderate and compassionate nature. Because of his constant defence and preservation of Emperor Hadrian's (76-138 A.D.) memory he gained the appellative of *Pious*. Apparently, during his long reign even the persecution of Christians was milder than before. Antoninus' economic policy was sound and cautious. He also used his personal patrimony in order to provide money to the people and to the soldiers. Among his many achievements in the field of public works, he completed the Mausoleum and the temples of Hadrian.. He also restored the *Colosseum*, the *Pons Sublicius*, and the *Graecostadium*. Antoninus' legislative activity, frequently cited in Justinian's *Digest*, brought about important innovations, especially in family and inheritance law.

12. These are important passages where Beccaria reaffirms his support of "enlightened despotism," as the only way to neutralize the power of the intermediary political bodies, such as the nobility and the clergy.

§ XXIX. Preventive Detention

1. That is, the confession before trial.

2. Here probably Beccaria refers to the Lombards, a Germanic barbaric population that settled in the Po valley in northern Italy A.D. 568.

3. According to Francioni (1984: 97, fn. 1), here Beccaria takes quite a radical position on territorial jurisdiction, stating that the crime should be prosecuted only in the State in which it has been committed. This would limit the possibility of bringing legal action against particularly dangerous offenders, particularly the ones guilty of the so-called "crimes against humanity."

4. Deportation for forced labor (i.e., to the Republic of Venice as galley slaves) was a frequent punishment in Beccaria's time, not to mention the great number of English convicts sent to colonies.

5. Matching the punishment to the crime is an essential feature of the retributive ideal, with ancient roots. Unless one exactly reproduces the crime in the punishment, however, it is virtually impossible to match the method of punishment with the method of the crime. i.e., should a rapist be raped? See: Newman (2008).

§ XXX. Criminal Proceedings and the Statute of Limitations

1. *prescrizione* in this context is a technical legal term meaning "statute of limitations," which is a statute (a law promulgated by the legislative branch of a government) fixing a period of time after which a given right cannot be enforced or an offense cannot be prosecuted.. This statute is similar, though not identical, to the statute of limitations used in common and civil law systems.

2. See: Chapter XXII, fn. 2. Beccaria was ambivalent concerning the right to and role of private property in society at one point calling it "a necessary right" and at another "an unnecessary right."

§ XXXI. Crimes Difficult to Prove

1. That is, pederasty.

2. Reminiscent of Montesquieu's view that sexual drives are strongly influenced by climate. See: Montesquieu (1949: passim).

3. A likely hint to Beccaria's conflict with his father, who strongly opposed his marriage to Teresa Blasco. See: Maestro (1973: 6-8).

4. Secret love affairs.

5. All-male institutions such as boarding schools and seminaries run by religious orders.

6. That is, sexual satisfaction.

7. Here probably Beccaria refers to the crimes of both infanticide and abortion.

§ XXXII. Suicide

1. *Sed, quis custodiet ipsos custodies?* (But, who will control the controllers themselves?) This is Juvenal's famous passage (Decimus Junius Juvenalis, *Satyrae*, II, 6). It is difficult to follow Beccaria's argument here. Having demonstrated the uselessness of a law against suicide, he then argues that all useless laws should be disposed of, followed by the observation that laws that control the borders of countries are also useless. This is perhaps an early recognition of globalization in the eighteenth century! However, it is not clear how this argument leads to his use of the famous expression "who will guard the guards?" unless we revert to his early criticism of legislation against suicide as turning the state into a prison, which is primarily an allegorical use of the word "prison." But in the following sentences he attempts to demonstrate that a state cannot really be a prison because it cannot (and should not) police its borders.

2.   This issue hides one very serious criticism of the social contract advanced by Hume who points out that the citizens of any country never choose to consent to that government since they are so far removed from its actual operations. In fact, he concludes it is the princes or sovereigns who make agreements with each other about how foreigners will be treated, especially when captured in war (Barker, 1947: 223).

3.   While material goods and possessions do not necessarily make men happy, they are necessary for the general well being of a nation to help alleviate the inevitable inequalities that arise in any nation where people live together in market economies.

4.   This appears to be part of Beccaria's nascent theory of population, economic well being and political freedom. He argues that the more people there are, the more difficult it is for a sovereign or national body to control them all, thus the more freedom they have. However, the quality of that freedom has to be tempered by the fact that where a sovereign or national body cannot scrutinize many people's lives, the freedom that they may enjoy will be conditioned by the extent to which they manage to extract material rewards from the market place. Beccaria seems to be saying that it is inevitable that possessions will end up in the hands of a few, yet at the same time this makes the rich dependent on the poor to contribute to the production of goods that the rich may enjoy. Thus a certain mutual dependence arises, so long as the rich do not become despotic rulers as well as being rich. Though not developed here, this view of population, happiness and the production of goods and services is consistent with Adam Smith's notion of the way in which an economy, motivated by individuals pursuing self interest, thrives because of that self interest and so in the long run benefits everyone, thus producing the "wealth of nations." By Smith's view, therefore, the more people in markets, the more wealth produced. The more trade across borders, the more wealth produced (Smith, 1776).

5.   See: Rousseau, Social Contract, III, Chapter 8.

6.   That is, despotic regimes will frighten away those who would otherwise contribute by their industry to the economic well being of the nation.

7.   That is, laws against emigration, and attempts to control borders that necessarily inhibit commerce.

§ XXXIII. Smuggling

1.   Human nature has been tamed over many centuries of violence, replaced by well established formalities that control it, such as the formalities of the criminal justice system. In Freudian terms, sublimation channels violence into seeming more rational pursuits and human endeavors. See: Introduction to the *Treatise*.

2.   See: Beccaria (1766), *Tentativo analitico su i contrabbandi,* in Francioni: 109, fn. 2. This observation is perhaps the first recognition of the opportunity theory of crime as well as the attractiveness of products to thieves. If there are long borders, there are more opportunities to cross them without being caught (poor surveillance); the goods if in small parcels are more easily removable; a high import tax creates an incentive for individuals to buy smuggled merchandise at a lower price, so the goods are more easily disposable. See: Clarke (1999) concerning items that are craved by thieves.

3.   The rational choice theory of crime. See: Cornish and Clarke (1987)

4.   Here, Beccaria reverts to the old idea of punishments "fitting the crime" by attempting to match the quality (not the quantity) of the punishment to the specific elements of the crime. It is also a "payback" a form of restitution in having the

offender serve the victim (in this case the royal treasury) to make up for what he stole. See: Newman (2008).

§ XXXIV. Debtors

1. See: Facchinei (1765). See: Chapter VII, fn. 1.
    See: Chapter VII, fn. 1.
2. Thus turning an innocent bankrupt into a fraudulent one.
3. Another obscure passage. According to Romagnoli the meaning of this sentence is that impunity is less dangerous for the public when the crime is difficult to ascertain. See: Beccaria (1994: 141, fn. 112).

§ XXXV. Sanctuaries

1. The right of asylum, still effective in some jurisdictions in Beccaria's time granted protection from arrest in religious buildings (monasteries and churches), especially for political refugees.
2. Extradition treaties.
3. Beccaria's fondness for irony has surely spawned this sentence: getting rid of sanctuaries because the idea that any lawful entity would condone crime is absurd.

§ XXXVI. Bounties

1. That is, in an enlightened and well organized society, fraud and trickery are more easily exposed and recognized.

§ XXXVII. Attempts, Accomplices, Pardons

1. See: Introduction to the *Treatise* and Chapter VII, fn. 1 for further discussion of Beccaria's contradictory view on criminal intent.
2. Difficult to understand: Since the executor's action has been determined only by this extra compensation allowed by the accomplices, the punishment should be the same for everybody (see: Francioni: 114, fn. 1).
3. This lyrical diatribe belies the basic principles that underlie much of Beccaria's essay: utilitarian principles, that is, the rational and logical means necessary to achieve the end, are the only way to overcome the many defects he identifies in the criminal justice system. There are many passages in his essay where Beccaria prescribes exactly what he here excoriates: the precise calculation of the amount of punishment for the corresponding crime, taking into account the utilitarian principle that the injury done by the punishment should exceed the injury of the crime by only the amount necessary to prevent the crime being committed in the future. This principle unavoidably excludes any consideration of the effects of the punishment on the offender, since his "welfare" must be subjected to the greater principle of utility for the common good. Thus, it is a "sacrifice" (a word Beccaria often uses to denigrate primitive punishments) of the offender for the common good. The difference in Beccaria's case however is that it uses cold, calm calculations to decide on the offender's punishment, the very method he criticizes in this passage. In contrast, the savage punishments Beccaria criticizes he says are sacrifices to the blood thirsty rabble. Surely it is clear throughout the essay that Beccaria categorically rejects the latter. So why should he indulge in rejecting his proposed alternative, the utilitarian principles of social control? One reason may be that Beccaria fails to carefully disentangle the rational methods needed to apply

the utilitarian solution to the criminal justice process and the formalities—closely resembling rituals (and indeed may become rituals)—that are needed to implement them. In Chapter XXXVIII Beccaria advocates exactly this.

§ XXXVIII. Suggestive Interrogations, Depositions

1. It is not clear how this could be achieved, especially given Beccaria's criticisms of formalities employed in the criminal justice process in Chapter XXXVII.
2. This is a puzzling sentence since it seems to open the door to torture which he roundly denounces in Chapter XVI, The essential *raison d'être* of torture is to get the accused to talk, and it is always his refusal that justifies an escalation of the punishment to harsh inflictions on the body. Thus, not only does Beccaria appear to approve of torture but also corporal punishment. (On the distinctions between torture and corporal punishment, see: Newman 1983). Having made fun of the grammar used by those who advocate suggestive interrogations, Beccaria seems to fall into the same trap.

§ XXXIX. On a Particular Kind of Crime

1. This vivid passage, according to Francioni (1984: 117 fn. 1) is almost directly taken from Verri (*Orazione panegirica sulla giurisprudenza milanese*)
2· The crime of heresy.
3. In this chapter (which is possibly made ambiguous by Beccaria, in order to avoid attacks from religious authorities) the author's argument is against the identification of sin with crime, derived from medieval juridical traditions and more generally against "opinion" crimes in religious matters. See: Introduction to the *Treatise* and Francioni (1984: 118, fn. 1).

§ XL. False Ideas of Utility

1. How much liberty are people prepared to give up in order to prevent crime? Beccaria, having argued forcefully throughout the *Treatise* in favor of preventing crimes rather than punishing them after they are committed, now takes a step back. He recognizes, as critics of situational crime prevention have argued recently (Garland, 2001) that taking the utilitarian notion of prevention to its extreme would result in an excessive curtailment of liberty in order to completely minimize risk—obviously an impossibility made clear by his excellent examples of fire and water. However, modern situational crime prevention assesses not an abstraction such as "liberty" but concrete inconveniences that may be caused by interventions. Taken in moderation, therefore, requiring fences around swimming pools, or children to wear life vests, or hotels to have fire alarm systems may be inconveniences, but are clearly well worth it considering the numbers of deaths prevented.
2. Beccaria here provides the basis for the most widely cited reason for the modern right to bear arms in the United States, the supporters of which claim it to be enshrined in the U.S. Constitution. The origins of this famous amendment in the Constitution are much debated, but there is little doubt that Beccaria's *Treatise* was consulted by the framers of the constitution, though probably not using Beccaria's argument since the right to bear arms was added as an amendment in 1789 based largely on the concern about citizenry being able to defend themselves against "maladministration"—the revolution still fresh in their minds. The origin of the clause, however, is very controversial. Certainly we know that both Jefferson and Adams owned copies of the *Treatise*, probably the Morellet translation. Much

research has been conducted to test Beccaria's claim that gun ownership prevents violent crime. There is no clear answer.

3. That is, too much control by laws turns men into lifeless things, takes away their motivation.

4. Beccaria seems to argue here against the idea of crime prevention because of its remoteness in time from instant events. Yet the idea of future goals to be achieved through means applied in the present is surely embedded in the very idea of utility, and a position that in other places Beccaria clearly supports as did the great utilitarians of the period, especially Bentham. The subsequent passages make clearer his concern: it is crime prevention through fear that he objects to, not so much crime prevention itself, though he does not explicitly say so here. The title of the following chapter holds hope that he will develop this idea further.

5. This may be a criticism of Hobbes who argued that the main motivator of humans was fear, and it was only fear, the sword, that would get humans to obey. See the Introduction to the *Treatise* for further discussion of Hobbes compared to Beccaria.

6. That is, despots or tyrants, though they are able to turn their subjects into slave like individuals, sow the seeds of their own destruction, since the resentment among those subjected to severe tyranny will inevitably erupt at first by a desperate act of an individual, then spontaneously will become a revolt: for the downtrodden have nothing to lose.

§ XLI. How to Prevent Crimes

1. The basic utilitarian principle stated, among many others, by Montesquieu (1949: VI, 9.) See also Introduction to the *Treatise*.

2. The idea of good and bad legislation is probably taken from Helvétius whose thoroughgoing utilitarianism probably set the framework for much of Beccaria's *Treatise*. Bad legislation is based on ideas that have no public utility, which, according to Helvétius, was religion, especially that of the Roman Catholic Church. "… the virtues and vices of the people depend upon the goodness and badness of the legislation, and that most moralities in the paintings they make of the vices seem less inspired by the love of the public welfare, than by personal interest and private hatred" (Helvétius, 1759: vii)

3. It is unfortunate that Beccaria, in this chapter that begins with such promise, confines his discussion of crime prevention as a function of law making, particularly prohibitions. This leads him to a number of interesting and indeed challenging propositions concerning the viability of using legislation to control crime. See: Introduction to the *Treatise* for a more detailed account of Beccaria's view of the relationship between law, human nature and crime prevention.

4. Thus inducing hope of impunity.

§ XLII. On the Sciences

1. See: Introduction to the *Treatise* for more discussion of Beccaria's notion of the sciences.

2. This passage can be interpreted as a probable refutation of Rousseau's view on arts and science as expounded in his *Discours sur les sciences et les arts*. See: Francioni (1984; 123 fn. 1).

3. This was the view widely held at the time of the simple savage who obeyed the

rituals of his tribe unquestioningly and without any sense of freedom, reproduced roughly later in Durkheim's concept of "mechanical solidarity." i.e., savages behaved without thinking, without any idea of "liberty." Much has been written on how or why the notion of liberty arose in humans. Beccaria seems here to opt for a simple explanation: the more people there were the more complicated social arrangements became, so one needed some way of formal regulation of individuals, thus the idea of "individual" is born; thus the idea of "individual liberty." The exact links in the logic of this explanation are obscure, complicated by Beccaria's failure to tell us when exactly impressions turned into thoughts, because without the latter, presumably there could be no idea of an "individual." Of course, the final epoch, according to Durkheim and anticipated by Beccaria, was the "scientific epoch." See: Introduction to the *Treatise* for further discussion of this perennial problem in social theory.

§ XLIV. Rewards

1.   This chapter leaves many questions unanswered, indeed, not asked. What is a reward exactly? Is it the opposite to punishment? One presumes that Beccaria sees rewards within the Benthamite pleasure-pain principle. But how does this work in a society, especially in regard to laws? It would seem to follow from Beccaria that laws should include in them rewards as well as punishments, otherwise surely the same evils of discretionary distribution of punishment would also apply to rewards? Which, under these circumstances one could imagine might become "bribes"? This chapter may also have spawned the book by one of Beccaria's contemporaries, Dragonetti (1766) *Delle Virtù e dei Premi* (On Virtues and Rewards), not a highly regarded book which remains mostly unknown today, though was popular in revolutionary America, cited often by Thomas Paine (who did not cite Beccaria, though much of what he cited looks very much like Beccaria's *Treatise*).
2.   Perhaps the failure of western law to emphasize virtue (in contrast to other systems of law such as Islamic law) is revealed by the well known expression "virtue is its own reward." The enlightenment thinkers were very critical of this idea, since they reveled in unveiling the hypocrisy of those held up to be most virtuous, who were almost always represented as characters of political or religious authority. Voltaire was probably the most influential critic of this false morality, both in his writings and in his famous legal cases, but the most scathing was the Marquis de Sade, in particular his novel *Justine* (1787) written while in prison.

§ XLV. Education

1.   Jean Jacques Rousseau, whose book *Emile* had been burned in public in 1762. This book formed the basis of liberal education as we would call it today—and still remains a challenging and radical approach to the education of the child that avoids punishment and emphasizes the child's self education through discovery as he explores the world around him.
2.   It is unclear to what "originals and copies" Beccaria refers. Given that Beccaria was apparently referring to Rousseau's *Emile* in the previous passage, he probably means that the child should learn from real moral events, that is, learn through experience, rather than have morality or even scientific facts formally taught him as a set of rules (copies of the real thing) which he must learn by rote, suffering punishment when he gets it wrong (discipline).

§ XLVII. Conclusion

1. Beccaria ends on a most optimistic note when he assumes that as society gains in sophistication the sensibilities of people will become more refined. Any student of history may question this sweeping assertion about the nature of human civilizations and of human nature in general. It certainly goes against much of Beccaria's commentaries on human nature in the early chapters of this essay, where on the contrary he describes human nature as essentially violent and that it is this violent nature that has to be overcome by legislation in order to reduce the severity of punishment. So while the famous concluding paragraph which follows sounds great—and it is—it is mired in deep contradictions, as we note in the Introduction to the *Treatise*.

References

Adams, H.P. (1935). *The Life and Writings of Giambattista Vico.* London: George Allen and Unwin.

Adams, John (1770) [1961]. *Diary and Autobiography of John Adams,* Volume I, The Belknap Press, Cambridge, MA (1961), pp. 352-54.

Bailyn, Bernard (1967). *The Ideological Origins of the American Revolution.* Cambridge, MA. The Belknap Press.

Bainton, Roland Herbert (1951). *Here I Stand; a Life of Martin Luther.* London: Hodder and Stoughton.

Barker, Ernest (1947). *Social Contract.* London: Oxford University Press.

Barker, Sir Ernest (1947). *Social Contract. Essays by Locke, Hume and Rousseau.* London: Oxford University Press.

Beccaria, Cesare (1762). *Del disordine e de' rimedi delle monete nello stato di Milano nell'anno 1762.* Lucca: Giuntini.

Beccaria, Cesare (1766). "Tentativo analitico su i contrabbandi". *Il Caffè,* Vol I, f. XV.

Beccaria, Cesare (1994). *Dei delitti e delle pene. Introduzione di Arturo Carlo Iemolo.* Torino: Biblioteca Universale Rizzoli.

Beccaria, Cesare (1995). *On Crimes and Punishments and Other Writings.* Translated and edited by, Richard Bellamy, Richard Davies and Virginia Cox. Cambridge: Cambridge University Press.

Beccaria, Cesare (1999). *Dei delitti e delle pene.* Introduzione di Arturo Carlo Iemolo. Torino: Biblioteca Universale Rizzoli.

Beirne, Piers (1991). Inventing Criminology: The "Science of Man" in Cesare Beccaria's Dei delitti delle pene (1764). *Criminology.* Volume 29, Number 4: 777-820.

Beirne, Piers (1993). *Inventing Criminology: Essays on the Rise of Homo Criminalis.* NY: State University of New York Press.

Bellamy, Richard, Richard Davies and Virginia Cox (Translator) (1995). *Beccaria: On Crimes and Punishments and Other Writings.* Cambridge: Cambridge University Press.

Benamati, Dennis, Phyllis Schultze, Graeme Newman and Adam Bouloukos (1997). *Handbook of Criminal Justice Information Sources.* Oryx Press.

Bentham, Jeremy (1948) [1789]. *Introduction to the Principles of Morals and Legislation.* New York: Hafner.

Bentham, Jeremy (1975). [1874] *The Theory of Legislation.* Oceana Publications Inc.

Bernard, Thomas J. (1983). *The Consensus-Conflict Debate: Form and Content in Social Theories.* New York: Columbia University Press.

Bierstedt, Robert. (1978). "Sociological Thought in the Eighteenth Century." in Tom Bottomore and Robert Nisbet (eds.) *A History of Sociological Analysis.* NY: Basic Books.

Blackstone, T. (1765). *Commentaries on the Laws of England,* first edition (Oxford: Clarendon Press.

Blackstone, T. (1853). *Commentaries on the Laws of England*. Book IV. NY: William Dean.

Bock, Kenneth (1978). "Theories of Progress, Development and Evolution," in Tom Bottomore and Robert Nisbet (eds.) *A History of Sociological Analysis*. NY: Basic Books.

Bryson, Gladys (1945). *Man and Society: The Scottish Inquiry of the Eighteenth Century*. Princeton, NJ: Princeton University Press.

Buckle, Stephen (1991). *Natural Law and the Theory of Property*. Oxford: Clarendon.

Campbell, James S., Joseph R. Sahid and David P. Stang (1970). *Law and Order Reconsidered; Report of the Task Force on Law and Law Enforcement to the National Commission on the Causes and Prevention of Violence*. New York, Bantam Books.

Cantù, Cesare (1862). *Beccaria e il Diritto Penale*, Florence: G. Barbera.

Caso, Adolph (1975). *America's Italian Founding Fathers*. Boston. Branden Press, Publishers.

Caso, Adolph (Ed.) (1983). *An Essay on Crimes and Punishments by Cesare Beccaria*. Boston, MA: Branden Publishing.

Chinard, Gilbert (1926). *The Commonplace Book of Thomas Jefferson*. Baltimore, MD: Johns Hopkins Press.

Clarke Ronald V. (1999). *Hot Products: Understanding, Anticipating and Reducing Demand for Stolen Goods*. Police Research Series, Paper 112. London: Home Office.

Comte, August (1877). *Cours de Philosophie Positive*, fourth edition, vol.4. Paris: Balliere et fils.

Condorcet, Marie Jean Antoine Nicolas de Caritat, Marquis de (1804). *Esquisse d'un Tableau historique des progress de l'esprit humain,* in his *Oeuvres completes*. Paris: Henrichs, vol. VIII.

Cornish, D., and Clarke, R.V. (Eds.). (1986). *The Reasoning Criminal*. New York: Springer-Verlag.

Cosmides, Leda and John Tooby. (1989). Evolutionary psychology and the generation of culture. *Ethology and Sociobiology*. Volume 10.

Darwin, Charles. (1871). *The Descent of Man and Selection in Relation to Sex*. London: Murray.

De Sade, Marquis, *Justine* (1787).

De Tocqueville, Alexis (1899). *Democracy in America*. Translated and revised by Henry Reeve. NY: Colophon.

Dennett, Daniel C. (1995). *Darwin's Dangerous Idea: Evolution and the Meanings of Life*. NY: Touchstone, Simon & Schuster.

Dragonetti, Giacinto (1766). *Delle Virtù e dei Premi*. English translation in 1777, *A Treatise on Virtues and Rewards*. Translator unknown. Johnson and Payne.

Durkheim, Emile (1893). *The Division of Labour in Society*, The Free Press reprint 1997.

Durkheim, Emile (1915). *The Elementary Forms of the Religious Life*, (1912, English translation by Joseph Swain: The Free Press, 1965; new translation by Karen E. Fields 1995.

Durkheim, Emile (1938). *Rules of Sociological Method*. eighth edition translated by Sarah A. Solovay and John H. Mueller. Glencoe: The Free Press.

Durkheim, Emile (1965). *The Elementary Forms of Religious Life*. translated by Joseph Ward Swain. NY: The Free Press.

Ewen, Stuart (1988). *All Consuming Images: The Politics of Style in Contemporary Culture*. New York: Basic Books.

Facchinei, Ferdinando (1765). *Note ed osservazioni sul Libro Dei Delitti e Delle Pene*, Venice: Jan.

Ferguson, Adam. (1782). *An Essay on the History of Civil Society.* Fifth ed. London: Printed for T. Caddell.

Ferri, Enrico (1921). *Relazione sul Progetto Preliminare di Codice Penale Italiano.* Ministry of Justice, Roma: L'Univeselle, Imprimerie, Polyglotte. English translation, *Report and Preliminary Project for an Italian Penal Code*, by Edgar Betts, English Chamber of Commerce-Rome Branch.

Firpo, Luigi. (1984). Bibliografia. Le edizioni italiane del "Dei delitti e delle pene" in *Edizione nazionale delle opere di Cesare Beccaria,* diretta da Luigi Firpo, Vol. I. Milano: Mediobanca.

Foucault M. (1961) [2001]. *Madness and Civilization: a History of Insanity in the Age of Reason.* NY: Routledge.

Foucault, M. (1977). *Discipline and Punish.* New York: Pantheon.

Francioni, Gianni. (a cura di). (1984). *Dei Delitti e Delle Pene,* in *Edizione Nazionale delle Opere di Cesare Beccaria,* Ed. Luigi Firpo, *Vol. I.* Milano: Mediobanca

Freud, Sigmund (1962). *Civilization and its Discontents.* Translated and edited by James Strachey. New York, W.W. Norton.

Garland, David (2001). *The Culture of Control: Crime and Social Order in Contemporary Society.* Chicago, IL: University of Chicago Press.

Gottschalk, Martin (2001). *Punishment and Evolution.* Doctoral Dissertation. University at Albany.

Gouldner, Alvin W. (1970). *The Coming Crisis in Western Sociology.* NY: Avon Books.

Grotius, H. (1625). *De Jure Belli ac Pacis Libri Tres.* translated by F.W.Kelsey. Carnegie endowment for international peace. NY: Oceana Publications, 1964, Bk. II, Chapter 2, sec. Ii. 4-5.

Gummere Richard M. (1963). *The American Colonial Mind and the Classical Tradition* Cambridge: Cambridge University Press.

Haakonssen, Knud (1996). Natural Law and Moral Philosophy. NY: Cambridge University Press.

Hart, H.L.A. (1982). *Essays on Bentham,* New York: Oxford University Press.

Hazard, Paul (1954). *European Thought in the Eighteenth Century, from Montesquieu to Lessing.* Translation from the original French by J. Lewis May. New Haven, CT: Yale University Press

Helvétius, Claude-Adrienne (1810) [1777]. *De l' homme: A Treatise on Man: His Intellectual Faculties and His Education.* translated by W. Hooper.

Helvétius, Claude-Adrienne (1758). *De l' esprit.* Paris: Durand.

Helvétius, Claude-Adrienne (1759). *De l' esprit or Essays on the Mind and its Several Faculties.* translated by William Mudford. London.

Hobbes, Thomas (1651) [1991]. *Leviathan.* Edited R. Tuck. Cambridge: Cambridge University Press.

Horkheimer, Max and Theodor W. Adorno (2002). *Dialectic of Enlightenment.* Edited by Gunzelin Schmid Noerr Translated by Edmund Jephcott. CA: Stanford University Press.

Horowitz, Irving (1954). *Claude Helvétius: Philosopher of Democracy and Enlightenment.* NY: Paine-Whitman.

Howard, Gregory J., Graeme R. Newman and William Pridemore (2000). "Theory, Method and Data in Comparative Criminology," in National Institute of Justice (Ed.) *Criminal Justice 2000: Measurement and Analysis of Crime and Justice.* Washington, D.C.: National Institute of Justice.

Hume, David (1947) [1748]. "Of the Original Contract." In Ernest Barker, Ed. *Social Contract.* London: Oxford University Press.

Hume, David (1999) [1748]. *An Enquiry Concerning Human Understanding.* sect. V, part II. London: Oxford University Press.

Hume, David (1967) [1739]. *A Treatise of Human Nature.* Oxford: Clarendon Press.

Hutcheson, Francis (1725). *An Inquiry into the Origin of our Ideas of Beauty and Virtue, in Two Treatises,* London: printed for D. Midwinter, A. Bettesworth, and C. Hitch.

Hutcheson, Francis (1755). *A System of Moral Philosophy.* Vol. II. London: A. Millar.

Inciardi, James A. (1984). *Criminal Justice.* Orlando, FL: Academic Press.

Jenkins, Philip (1984). "Varieties of Enlightenment Criminology: Beccaria, Godwin, de Sade," *British Journal of Criminology,* 24 (2): 112-30, (April).

Kimball, Marie (1943). *Jefferson: The Road to Glory, 1743 to 1776.* New York: Coward-McCann.

Koenig, Bernie (2004). Natural Law, Science, and the Social Construction of Reality. NY: University Press of America.

Kropotkin, Peter (1972). *Mutual Aid, a Factor of Evolution.* Edited and with an introduction by Paul Avrich. London: Allen Lane.

Laslett, P. (Ed.) (1949). *Patriarcha and other Political Works of Sir Robert Filmer.* Oxford: Basil Blackwell.

Lely, Gilbert (1970). *The Marquis de Sade*, translated by Alex Brown, New York: The Free Press.

Lenin, V.I. (1918). *State and Revolution.* translated by Robert Service. London: Penguin Classics. 1993.

Lundberg, David and Henry May (1976). "The Enlightened Reader in America," *American Quarterly* 28: 262–93.

Lutz, Donald S. (1984). "The Relative Influence of European Writers on Late Eighteenth Century American Political Thought," *American Political Science Review,* 78: 189–97.

Maestro, Marcello R. (1973). *Cesare Beccaria and the Origins of Penal Reform.* Philadelphia, PA: Temple University Press.

Maguire, Eduard, Graeme R. Newman, and Gregory J. Howard (1998). "Measuring the Performance of National Criminal Justice Systems." *Journal of Comparative and Applied Criminology.* Spring, 22.

Manzoni, Alessandro (1840). *I Promessi Sposi./ Storia Milanese del Secolo XVII.* Edizione riveduta dall'autore, *Storia della Colonna Infame.* Milano: Guglielmini e Redaell.

Marongiu, Pietro and Graeme R. Newman (1997), "Situational crime prevention and the utilitarian tradition," In Graeme R. Newman, Ronald V. Clarke and Shlomo Shoham, (Eds.) *Foundations of Situational Crime Prevention Theory.* Dartmouth Press, 1997.

Marongiu, Pietro and Graeme R. Newman (1987). *Vengeance: The Fight against Injustice.* New Jersey: Littlefield & Adams.

Marx, Karl. (1934). *Capital.* New York: E.P. Dutton Co.

Mill, J. S. (1891). *Utilitarianism.* London and New York: Longmans Green.

Montesquieu, Charles L. de Secondat. (1748). *De l'Esprit des Loix.* Genève: Barillot & Fils.

Montesquieu, Charles L. de Secondat. (1901). *Persian Letters.* translated by John Davidson. NY: M.W.Dunne.

Montesquieu, Charles L. de Secondat. (1949). *The Spirit of Laws.* translated by Thomas Nugent. NY: Hafner Publishing.

Mullett, Charles F. (1939-40). "Classical Influences on the American Revolution," *Classical Journal,* 35, 93, 94.

Newman, Graeme R. (1983). *Just and Painful: A Case for the Corporal Punishment of Criminals.* NY: Macmillan. The Free Press.

Newman, Graeme R. (2008). *The Punishment Response*. Second edition NJ: Transaction.

Newman, Graeme R. and Pietro Marongiu (1990). "Penological reform and the myth of Beccaria". *Criminology*. Volume 28, Number 2, May.

Newman, Graeme R. and Pietro Marongiu (1997). "Situational crime prevention and the utilitarian theories of Jeremy Bentham," In Graeme Newman, Ronald Clarke and Shlomo Shoham, (Eds.) *Rational Choice and Situational Crime Prevention..* Dartmouth: Ashgate.

Newman, Graeme R. and Pietro Marongiu (1997). "Situational crime prevention and the utilitarian tradition, In Graeme R. Newman, Ronald V. Clarke and Shlomo Shoham, (Eds.) *Foundations of Situational Crime Prevention Theory*. Dartmouth Press.

Paine, Thomas (1776). *Common Sense*. Philadelphia.

Paolucci, H. (translator) (1963). Introduction. *Beccaria: On Crimes and Punishments*. New York: Bobbs-Merrill.

Passerin d'Entrèves, Alexander (1994). *Natural Law: An Introduction to Legal Philosophy*. New Brunswick, NJ: Transaction Publishers.

Pufendorf, S. (1672). *De Jurum Naturae ad Gentium Libri Octo*. translated by C.H. and W.A. Oldfather, NY: Oceana Publications.

Ridley, Matt. (1996). *The Origins of Virtue*. London: Penguin.

Robertson, John (2008). *The Scottish Contribution to the Enlightenment*. http://www. history.ac.uk/eseminars/sem12.html

Romangoli, Sergio, (Ed.) *Cesare Beccaria: Opere,* Sansoni Superbiblioteca, Volume 1., p. xxiv.

Rousseau, Jean Jaques. (1930). *Emile*. translated by Barbara Fox. London: Everyman's Library, J.M. Dent and Sons.

Rousseau, Jean Jaques. (1947). *The Social Contract and Discourse*. translated and with an introduction by G.D.H. Cole. London: Everyman's Library, J.M. Dent and Sons.

Saint-Simon, Henri de (1964). *Social Organisation, the Science of Man and Other Writings*. F. Markham, ed. New York: Harper & Row.

Sellin, T. and M.E. Wolfgang (1964). *The Measurement of Delinquency*. New York: John Wiley.

Sellin, Thorsten. (1976). *Slavery and the Penal System*, NY: Elsevier.

Smith, Adam. 1976 [1776]. *An Inquiry into the Nature and Causes of the Wealth of Nations*. Ed. R. H. Campbell and A.S. Skinner. Oxford: Clarendon.

Smith, D.W. (1965). *Helvétius: A Study in Persecution*. Oxford: Clarendon.

Teggart, Frederick J. (1949). *The Idea of Progress: A Collection of Readings*. Revised edition Introduction by George H. Hildebrande. Berkeley and Los Angeles: University of California Press.

Tuck, Richard (Ed.) (1991). Hobbes: Leviathan, Cambridge: Cambridge University Press.

Turgot, Anne-Robert-Jacques, Baron de Laune (1913). "Tableau philosophique des progress successifs de l'esprit humain," and "Plan de deux sur l'histoire universalle," in Gustave Schelle (ed.) *Oeuvres de Turgot et Documents le Concernant*. Paris: F. Alcan.

United States. President's Commission on Law Enforcement and Administration of Justice. (1967). *The Challenge of Crime in a Free Society*. Washington, U.S. Government Printing Office.

Valeri, Nino (1969). *Pietro Verri,* Florence: Felice le Monnier.

Venturi, Franco (1960). 'Les lumieres dans l'Europe du 18e siecle', first published in *XIe Congres. International des Sciences Historiques: Rapports*, IV, Histoire Moderne (Stockholm, 1960); translated into English as 'The European Enlightenment', in S.J.

Woolf (ed), Franco Venturi, *Italy and the Enlightenment. Studies in a Cosmopolitan Century* (London, 1972). *Utopia and Reform in the Enlightenment* (Cambridge, 1971)

Venturi, Franco (Ed.). (1999). *Cesare Beccaria, Dei delitti e delle pene. Con una raccolta di lettere e documenti relativi alla nascita dell'opera e alla sua fortuna nell'Europa del Settecento.* Torino: Einaudi.

Verri, Pietro (1988) [1776]. *Osservazioni sulla Tortura,* Milano: Rizzoli.

Verri, Pietro (1766). *Meditazioni sulla felicità.* Milano: Galeazzi.

Vico, Giambattista (1725). *Principi di una scienza nuova d'intorno alla commune natura delle nazioni* (Principles of a new science concerning the common nature of nations) in [1961]. Thomas Goddard Bergin and Max Harold Frisch, trans.*The New Science.* Garden City, NY: Anchor Books, Doubleday and Co.

Vold, George B. and Thomas J. Bernard (1986). *Theoretical Criminology.* third edition New York: Oxford University Press.

Weinreb, Lloyd L. (1987). *Natural Law and Justice.* Cambridge, MA: Harvard University Press.

Wooton, Barbara (1959). *Social Science and Social Pathology.* New York: Macmillan Company.

Wootton. David (2000). "Helvétius: From Radical Enlightenment to Revolution." *Political Theory,* Volume 28, No. 3, (June), pp. 307-36.

Young, David B. (1983). "Cesare Beccaria: Utilitarian or Retributivist? *Journal of Criminal Justice,* 11: 317-26.

Young, David B. (1986). *Beccaria: On Crimes and Punishments.* Indiana: Hackett.